TABLE OF CONTENTS

➤━➤▸-◉-◂◄━◄

➤━➤▸-◉-◂◄━◄

Unless otherwise indicated, all Scripture quotations are taken from the King James Version of the Bible.

7 Keys To One Thousand Times More
ISBN 1-56394-093-0/B-104
Copyright © 1998 by *MIKE MURDOCK*
All publishing rights belong exclusively to Wisdom International
Published by The Wisdom Center
P. O. Box 99 • Denton, Texas 76202 • 1-888-WISDOM-1 (1-888-947-3661)
Website: www.thewisdomcenter.tv

SPECIAL DEDICATION TO ORAL AND EVELYN ROBERTS.

▶ You are the Patriarchs of Miracles and Blessings.

▶ Your presence has unleashed a million miracles for my generation.

▶ You are the first I ever heard obsessed in declaring that God is truly a *good* God.

▶ You are the first and only champions who ever told me God wanted to increase me *One Thousand Times More.*

▶ You are the Uncommon Man and Woman of God, Oral and Evelyn Roberts, who unveiled for me the Golden Gate called Increase.

I dedicate this written revelation of, *"7 Keys To One Thousand Times More."*

My heart is filled with gratitude and indebtedness to both of you.

-MIKE MURDOCK

Why I Wrote This Book

It really happened on a Sunday morning.

One of my most treasured staff members, Monica Melgar, left this message on my voice mail: "Dr. Oral Roberts is speaking at my church Sunday morning. Since he is one of your favorite Mentors, I thought you would try to go since this is your only Sunday off this year."

It was Christmas. My schedule stays over-loaded, so, I had decided to use this weekend off for personal restoration and renewing. The beloved pastors of Covenant Church, Mike and Kathy Hayes, had invited Dr. Roberts to speak in their church here in Dallas.

No thinking man would stay home when Oral Roberts is in town. So, I attended.

I have listened to Oral Roberts for years. He has become my personal friend and Mentor. His life has affected me more than almost anyone in my lifetime. Nobody walks with more compassion and integrity. He is obsessed with doing the will of God.

Several weeks before, one of my dearest friends, Frank Berry, had telephoned me: "Have you heard Oral Robert's teaching on the *One Thousand Times More* Blessing?" I had not.

Laughingly, I told Frank that I was just begin-ning to grasp an understanding of the 100-fold blessing Jesus promised to those who followed Him (read Mark 10:28-30).

When I went to Covenant Church, Dr. Roberts spoke on that very topic, *"A Thousand Times More!"* He related how God wanted to bless Israel. He explained that miracles, signs and wonders were the methods God used to communicate His love and caring. He shared God's glorious promise to those who dared use their faith. He used a text that I had passed over numerous times. *(Others often see things we never see.)* He read aloud to us:

"The Lord your God hath multiplied you, and, behold, ye are this day as the stars of heaven for multitude. The Lord God of your fathers make you *a thousand times so many more* as ye are, and bless you, as He hath promised you!" (Deuteronomy 1:10, 11).

I wish I could remember everything he taught us that morning, but my mind was exploding with memories of the goodness of God in my own life. Often, I had heard Oral Roberts declare these unchanging truths repeatedly:

"God is a good God!"

"Something good is going to happen to you!"

"Expect a miracle!"

Few ministers are this obsessed with the *goodness* of God. Many leaders have become *consumed with the depravity of man, the deceit of satan,* and the inevitable tragedies that follow disobedience.

Oral Roberts is consumed with the *goodness and greatness of our God.*

While he spoke that morning, my heart overflowed with the golden memories of God's goodness. It is true, God is a very good God. He wants our *increase*. He is not a thief, but a Giver. He does not desire to *destroy* us, but to *protect* us. He pursues our good. He schedules our miracles. He delights in every moment of uncommon faith.

After the service, my father and I had a private lunch with Dr. Roberts, Mike and Kathy Hayes. It was a glorious and precious day. As I talked with my Mentor, something rose up like a holy mist within me—a desire to bless him and sow into his dominant Dream and vision.

Uncommon Men Unlock *Uncommon Seeds.*

Uncommon Men Unlock *Uncommon Harvests.*

I told Dr. Roberts that I wanted to plant a very uncommon Seed into his life and ministry. He suggested mailing it, but I felt a surging desire to personally place it in his hands. I agreed to meet him at his hotel just before he flew out of D/FW Airport. It took over an hour to go to my office and prepare the check for sowing. I called his hotel room, and he came down to the lobby where we prayed over the *Seed.* As we prayed, he asked me the most pressing needs of my life. I had two. I shared the dominant one. I knew that he wanted me to give my Seed an Assignment. Every *Seed* should be *aimed like an arrow* toward a desired target of need—the greatest Harvest desired. Then, he insisted that I would not come out of our agreement together for the Harvest. I nodded. But, he insisted I speak it *aloud.*

"I am not coming out of the agreement for my Harvest."

When I spoke those words aloud, something supernatural birthed. I knew it without a doubt.

Something had shifted in the Spirit world toward my life. Something wonderful and favorable. When God reaches for you, satan cannot effectively stand between Him and you. I did not know *how* my desired Harvest would come. Neither did I know *where* God would begin blessing me first. Wisdom? Favor? Relationships? Finances? I simply did not know. But, I did know *"something good was going to happen to me!"*

Within a few hours, a special telephone call came. One of my dear pastor friends in Florida was exploding with excitement. He had just received one of my monthly books in the mail, *Secrets of the Journey, Volume 5.* (I mail thousands of books each month to people who are obsessed with the Wisdom of God. It is my *Seed* into my generation. If you want to receive my monthly book, simply write and request it.)

"Mike, I love this book! I want to teach my people from this book. I want to feature it on my television program next week. Will you rush me 2,000 more copies?" Would I ever!

My one book became 2,000...within hours.

Two thousand books...planted into 2,000 families.

Two thousand families are now teaching their children from one of my books!

The Promise of *One Thousand Times More.*

A few weeks later, one of my staff informed me that a young lady was waiting outside my office. She wanted to personally bless my ministry. When she entered, she handed me a beautifully wrapped gift box saying, "God told me to plant this into your ministry and present it to you like this."

I opened the box. There before my eyes was $25,000 cash—the same amount of the *Seed* I had placed in the hands of the man of God, Dr. Oral Roberts. It had already been *given back* to me.

The Promise of *One Thousand Times More* had already begun.

Something within you *requires* increase.

You cannot *change* it.

You cannot *fast* it away.

You cannot *pray* it away.

Increase is deep within the heart and soul of every living thing. Even trees multiply! Birds multiply! Humans multiply! *Every living thing* multiplies!

The whole earth is pregnant.

The earth is pregnant with desire for increase.

It is not a *man* thing.

It is not a *satanic* thing.

Increase is a *God* thing.

Business leaders invest thousands of dollars in seminar education to increase the flow of their business. Clergymen fly across continents to be Mentored in the principles that increase the influence of their ministry or size of their congregation. Television programs are crammed with advertisements promising the secrets of *increase*—increasing your self-confidence, your ability to memorize, the profits from real estate transactions, and even increasing the joy of your marriage. *Every product promoted promises increase.*

Increase is the driving force of every living thing on earth.

Adam and Eve possessed a desire for increase before their fall into sin.

The serpent (satan) initiated the conversation. He appealed to an invisible need within them for knowledge, *increasing* their Wisdom and knowledge. "You shall not surely die: For God doth know that in the day ye eat thereof, then your eyes shall be opened, and ye shall be as gods, knowing good and evil." Then the Bible explains, "And when the woman saw that the tree was good for food, and that it was pleasant to the eyes, and a tree to be desired to make one wise, she took of the fruit" (read Genesis 3:4-6).

Satan had never seen a human before.

He had no idea what God had created.

He only could observe the fascination God had with the new loves of His life, Adam and Eve.

He stared enviously as God walked through the Garden of Eden, discussing His thoughts, plans and ideas with His new creation, man and woman. Imagine satan, hiding behind those bushes, in the form of a serpent, jealous, resentful and angry.

Satan knew God.

He knew the *nature* of God, *giving.*

He knew the *goal* of God, *relationship.*

He knew the *desire* of God, *increase.*

He knew the *pleasure* of God, *faith.*

He was fascinated with the gifts God possessed—power, creativity, authority and increase. Lacking those gifts tormented him. It angered and confused him. So, he attempted to dethrone God to assume the authority of God.

He lost everything because of it. *Everything.*

Observing God enjoying Adam and Eve tormented his heart. He knew that increase was in their future.

Now, satan did not entrap Adam and Eve with the lie, "God does not really love you." They already knew better. Satan did not attempt to persuade them that God did not *enjoy* them. God walked with them every day.

Satan deceived them by insinuating and implying that God resented their increase of knowledge and Wisdom. "For God doth know that in the day ye eat thereof, then your eyes shall be opened, and ye shall be as gods, knowing good and evil" (Genesis 3:5).

Satan is still effectively marketing this same devastating lie today.

Millions of Christians are still blinded to the desires of God to *give them increase.* Vows of poverty are presumed to impress God. The opposite occurs. God is only impressed by *faith,* not self-destruction.

The desire for increase was planted within you before your very birth. It is the *nature of God* within you—the nature of a *Multiplier.*

Your Heavenly Father is the Force of Increase in this universe.

You are His child, containing His very nature.

Yet, the Master Thief still lives on earth today —satan.

Satan studies anything God loves. He envies God. He is jealous of God. He is baffled and angry because of his inability to dethrone God. You see, anything that receives the attention of God inevitably receives the attention of satan. Job is an example. When satan appeared in the presence of God, God reminded him of Job and the pleasure He received from Job. Satan was so angry, he reacted (read Job 2:1-7).

Satan despises The Blessed.

Satan has never been able to remove that desire for increase from mankind. The most demonized man on earth still desires increase! So, satan uses that very approach to destroy the plans of God for your continual, explosive and miraculous increase.

6 Satanic Deceptions Concerning Increase

1.   He creates *doubt* that God wants you to experience increase.

2.   He creates *guilt* for even desiring increase. (Thousands of diligent workers are accused of being greedy and materialistic because of their constant pursuit of excellence.)

3.   He creates an attitude of *self-sufficiency.* Many attempt uncommon success without the counsel and assistance of God.

4.   He creates *jealousy* toward others who enjoy uncommon blessing. Envy is deadly.

5.   He creates an *inordinate desire* for something you have not yet earned or deserved. "Withhold not good from them *to whom it is due,* when it is in the power of thine hand to do it" (Proverbs 3:27).

6.   He tempts you to pursue increase *unlawfully or unethically.* Resenting your potential

increase, satan crafts brilliant strategies to para-lyze the Promise of *One Thousand Times More.* Yes, it is impossible for satan to expel your desire for increase.   Even babies reach for something more. He can only distort, pervert and twist this principle in your life. Through guilt, doubt and envy, he weaves a web of deceit that robs you of the *One Thousand Times More* God said you deserved.

Poverty is so unnecessary.

Loss is so painful.

Ignorance is so deadly.

Wisdom is so rewarding.

I have fallen in love with the Holy Spirit. He is the Spirit of Wisdom (see Isaiah 11:2). He is the Source of every good gift you receive from God (read 1 Corinthians 2:9,10).

One Thousand Times More Peace.

One Thousand Times More Joy.

One Thousand Times More Love.

One Thousand Times More Finances.

One Thousand Times More Wisdom.

One Thousand Times More Miracles.

One Thousand Times More Victories.

One Thousand Times More Favor.

One Thousand Times More Ideas.

I know your *need* for increase, your *desire* for increase, your *Source* for increase.

I hate pain.

Your pain can stop.

I want you *completely healed.*

That is why I wrote this book.

-MIKE MURDOCK

The Seasons
Of Your Life
Will Change
Every Time You Decide
To Use Your Faith.

-MIKE MURDOCK

≈ 1 ≈

Know The True Source Of Increase.

━━━━◆━━━━

Everything Comes From Somewhere.
Everything comes from Someone.
Everything Comes From God. "For by Him were all things created, that are in heaven, and that are in earth, visible and invisible, whether they be thrones, or dominions, or principalities, or powers: all things were created by Him, and for Him: And He is before all things, and by Him all things consist" (Colossians 1:16,17).

How Much Blessing Is Really Enough?

God is even interested in your financial increase.

Here Are 7 Reasons God Wants To Increase Your Finances

1.   *God Wants You To Have Enough Finances To Provide An Uncommon And Wonderful Income For Your Spiritual Leaders And Pastors.* "Let the elders that rule well be counted worthy of double honour, especially they who labour in the word and doctrine. For the scripture saith, Thou shalt not muzzle the ox that treadeth out the corn. And, The

labourer is worthy of his reward" (1 Timothy 5:17, 18).

2. *God Wants You To Have Enough Finances To Send Ministers Throughout The World Preaching The Gospel.* "And how shall they preach, except they be sent? as it is written, How beautiful are the feet of them that preach the gospel of peace, and bring glad tidings of good things!" (Romans 10:15).

3. *God Desires To Provide Enough Finances For You To Pay Your Taxes And Obligations.* "Render therefore unto Caesar the things which are Caesar's; and unto God the things that are God's" (Matthew 22:21).

4. *God Desires You To Have Enough Finances To Return The Tithe Back To His House That Belongs To The Work Of God.* "And all the tithe of the land, whether of the seed of the land, or of the fruit of the tree, is the Lord's: it is holy unto the Lord" (Leviticus 27:30).

5. *God Desires You To Have Enough Finances To Give Good And Uncommon Gifts To Your Children And Those You Love.* "If ye then, being evil, know how to give good gifts unto your children, how much more shall your Father which is in heaven give good things to them that ask Him?" (Matthew 7:11).

6. *God Desires You To Have Enough Finances To Help The Poor.* "He that hath pity upon the poor lendeth unto the Lord; and that which he hath given will He pay him again" (Proverbs 19:17).

7. *God Desires You To Have Enough Money To Solve Any Emergency Or Crisis That Arises.*

"...money answereth all things" (Ecclesiastes 10:19).

31 Important Facts You Should Know About Your True Source

Fools do not recognize the Holy Spirit as the Source. "The fool hath said in his heart, There is no God" (Psalm 14:1). But, increase of *One Thousand Times More* has to come from Someone Great...God.

1. *God Loves Being Your Daily Source.* "Blessed be the Lord, who daily loadeth us with benefits, even the God of our salvation" (Psalm 68:19).

2. *God Loves Giving To You.* "If ye then, being evil, know how to give good gifts unto your children, how much more shall your Father which is in heaven give good things to them that ask Him?" (Matthew 7:11).

3. *God Promised To Be A Sufficient And Capable Source And Provider.* "Wherefore, if God so clothe the grass of the field, which to day is, and to morrow is cast into the oven, shall He not much more clothe you, O ye of little faith?" (Matthew 6:30).

4. *God Promised To Be A Source Of Blessing And Wealth To Those Who Feared Him.* "Blessed is the man that feareth the Lord,...Wealth and riches shall be in his house: and his righteousness endureth for ever" (Psalm 112:1,3).

5. *God Is The Source Of Every Gift You Receive.* "Every good gift and every perfect gift is from above, and cometh down from the Father of

lights, with Whom is no variableness, neither shadow of turning" (James 1:17).

6. *The Holy Spirit Is The Gift Of God To You.* "Then Peter said unto them, Repent, and be baptized every one of you in the name of Jesus Christ for the remission of sins, and ye shall receive the gift of the Holy Ghost" (Acts 2:38).

7. *The Holy Spirit Created You.* "The Spirit of God hath made me, and the breath of the Almighty hath given me life" (Job 33:4).

8. *The Holy Spirit Is The Giver Of Every Other Gift You Receive.* "Eye hath not seen, nor ear heard, neither have entered into the heart of man, the things which God hath prepared for them that love Him. But God hath revealed them unto us by His Spirit: for the Spirit searcheth all things, yea, the deep things of God" (1 Corinthians 2:9,10).

9. *The Holy Spirit Decides The Various Gifts You Receive.* "Now there are diversities of gifts, but the same Spirit....For to one is given by the Spirit the word of wisdom; to another the word of knowledge by the same Spirit; To another faith by the same Spirit; to another the gifts of healing by the same Spirit; To another the working of miracles;" (read 1 Corinthians 12:4,8-10).

10. *The Holy Spirit Is The Source Of More Love For Others.* "...because the love of God is shed abroad in our hearts by the Holy Ghost which is given unto us" (Romans 5:5).

The Assignment of the Holy Spirit includes the birthing of uncommon love and compassion toward others. That love is not dependent on the behavior or conduct of others. It is a Divine deposit within you.

6 Qualities Of The Uncommon Love Of The Spirit

▶ *Uncommon Love Pursues.* "For the Son of man is come to seek and to save that which was lost" (Luke 19:10).

▶ *Uncommon Love Protects.* "...for I the Lord thy God am a jealous God," (Exodus 20:5). God said He would fight for you!

▶ *Uncommon Love Provides.* "...for your heavenly Father knoweth that ye have need of all these things. But seek ye first the kingdom of God, and His righteousness; and all these things shall be added unto you" (Matthew 6:32,33).

▶ *Uncommon Love Heals And Mends.* "...for I am the Lord that healeth thee" (Exodus 15:26).

▶ *Uncommon Love Is The Fruit Of The Spirit.* "But the fruit of the Spirit is love," (Gal. 5:22).

▶ *Uncommon Love Gives.* "For God so loved the world, that He gave His only begotten Son, that whosoever believeth in Him should not perish, but have ever lasting life" (John 3:16).

11. *The Holy Spirit Is Your True Source For One Thousand Times More Power.* "But ye shall receive power, after that the Holy Ghost is come upon you: and ye shall be witnesses unto Me both in Jerusalem, and in all Judaea, and in Samaria, and unto the uttermost part of the earth" (Acts 1:8).

12. *The Holy Spirit Requires Your*

Recognition Of Him. "Remember now thy Creator in the days of thy youth, while the evil days come not, nor the years draw nigh, when thou shalt say, I have no pleasure in them;" (Ecclesiastes 12:1).

13. *Your Dependency Upon The Holy Spirit Is Evidenced By The Peace In Your Life Concerning Your Provision.* If you are truly trusting the Holy Spirit as your true Source, you will nurture your relationship with Him.

If you are bitter toward your ex-husband and blaming him for your financial condition, you subconsciously believe that he should be your true source for supply.

If you have become embittered toward your employer because he did not give you an anticipated raise, you are depending on your employer as your true source of income.

Your words are revealing who you are really trusting. Your disappointment in people is evidence that you have been expecting from people, not God.

You will become embittered and retaliatory if you believe that your ex-mate or family has stopped the financial flow into your life.

You will become disillusioned and despondent if you believe that your IQ and gifts alone are responsible for your present financial losses.

But, you will unleash remarkable and uncommon joy when you embrace the golden fact that Jehovah-Jireh is the personal God of your life—the true Source of everything you need.

14. *The Holy Spirit Is The Source Of Every Good Thing In Your Life.* "...no good thing will He

withhold from them that walk uprightly" (Psalm 84:11).

15. *The Holy Spirit Is The Source Of Every Success, Idea, Gift Or Concept That Can Generate Wealth.* "But thou shalt remember the Lord thy God: for it is He that giveth thee power to get wealth, that He may establish His covenant which He swear unto thy fathers, as it is this day" (Deuteronomy 8:18).

16. *Your Obedience To The Holy Spirit Guarantees Uncommon Blessing And Increase.* "If ye be willing and obedient, ye shall eat the good of the land:" (Isaiah 1:19).

17. *The Holy Spirit Is A Person.* He is not fire. He is not rain. He is not a cloud. He is not a white bird, or dove. He is not an "it." He is a Person. Jesus trusted Him to finish what He started within us: "And I will pray the Father, and He shall give you another Comforter, that He may abide with you for ever;" (John 14:16).

18. *The Holy Spirit Is The Author Of The Word Of God.* "For the prophecy came not in old time by the will of man: but holy men of God spake as they were moved by the Holy Ghost" (2 Peter 1:21).

The Word of God, the *sword* of the Spirit, was used by Jesus as a *weapon* during times of crisis. "And Jesus answered him, saying, It is written, That man shall not live by bread alone, but by every Word of God" (Luke 4:4; see also Ephesians 6:17).

19. *The Holy Spirit Is The Earthly Intercessor Who Prays For You Daily.* "Likewise the

Spirit also helpeth our infirmities: for we know not what we should pray for as we ought: but the Spirit itself [Himself] maketh intercession for us with groanings which cannot be uttered. And He that searcheth the hearts knoweth what is the mind of the Spirit, because He maketh intercession for the saints according to the will of God" (Romans 8:26,27).

20. *The Holy Spirit Provides A Personal Prayer Language That Nobody Understands But Your Heavenly Father.* "For he that speaketh in an unknown tongue speaketh not unto men, but unto God: for no man understandeth him;" (1 Corinthians 14:2).

21. *When You Pray In The Holy Spirit, Using Your Prayer Language, It Will Multiply And Increase Your Personal Confidence And Strength In God.* "But ye, beloved, building up yourselves on your most holy faith, praying in the Holy Ghost, Keep yourselves in the love of God, looking for the mercy of our Lord Jesus Christ unto eternal life" (Jude 20,21).

22. *The Holy Spirit Decides Your Assignment —The Problem You Were Created To Solve For Others.* "Before I formed thee in the belly, I knew thee; and before thou camest forth out of the womb I sanctified thee, and I ordained thee a prophet unto the nations" (Jeremiah 1:5).

23. *The Holy Spirit Knows Where Your Knowledge, Gifts And Skills Are Most Needed.* "Then the Spirit said unto Philip, Go near, and join thyself to this chariot" (Acts 8:29).

24. *The Holy Spirit Chooses The Geographical Location Where You Will Flourish And Prosper.*

"As they ministered to the Lord, and fasted, the Holy Ghost said, Separate me Barnabas and Saul for the work whereunto I have called them. And when they had fasted and prayed, and laid their hands on them, they sent them away. So they, being sent forth by the Holy Ghost, departed unto Seleucia; and from thence they sailed to Cyprus" (Acts 13:2-4).

25. *The Holy Spirit Loves Singing.* "...come before His presence with singing" (Psalm 100:2). The Apostle Paul understood this, "I will sing with the Spirit, and I will sing with the understanding also" (1 Corinthians 14:15).

Old Testament leaders understood the power of singing. "And it came to pass, when the evil spirit from God was upon Saul, that David took an harp, and played with his hand: so Saul was refreshed, and was well, and the evil spirit departed from him" (1 Samuel 16:23).

26. *The Holy Spirit Often Uses Singing As a Weapon During Seasons Of Battle And Warfare.* "And when they began to sing and to praise, the Lord set ambushments against the children of Ammon, Moab, and mount Seir, which were come against Judah; and they were smitten" (2 Chronicles 20:22). Sing songs of remembrance, victory and anticipation of God's intervention in your life. Teach your children to sing, knowing singing is a secret weapon during times of crisis.

27. *The Holy Spirit Often Withdraws When He Is Offended By Our Conversation And Conduct.* "Let no corrupt communication proceed out of your mouth, but that which is good to the use of edifying, that it may minister grace unto the hearers.

And grieve not the Holy Spirit of God,...Let all bitterness, and wrath, and anger, and clamour, and evil speaking, be put away from you," (read Ephesians 4:29-31).

28. *When He Withdraws It Seems That His Manifest Presence Is Not As Obvious.* When He is grieved, He withholds His total peace, His joy, and inner rest. Confusion and restlessness are often the signs that the Holy Spirit has been grieved by us. "I will go and return to My place, till they acknowledge their offence," (Hosea 5:15).

29. *Uncommon Men Of God Trust God To Increase Them.* The prophet Samuel recognized it. "It is the Lord that advanced Moses and Aaron, and that brought your fathers up out of the land of Egypt" (1 Samuel 12:6).

30. *All Promotion Comes From God.* "For promotion cometh neither from the east, nor from the west, nor from the south. But God is the judge: He putteth down one, and setteth up another" (Psalm 75:6,7).

31. *The Holy Spirit Unlocks The Law Of Recognition.* Everything You Need Is Already In Your Life, Merely Awaiting Your Recognition Of It.

▶ Recognition of Your own dominant Gift.

▶ Recognition of the Gifts within Others.

▶ Recognition of the Voice of God.

▶ Recognition of an Enemy.

▶ Recognition of a Financial Deliverer.

▶ Recognition of your own Weakness.

▶ Recognition of a God-sent Mentor.

▶ Recognition of your Assignment.

▶ Recognition of an Uncommon Opportunity.

▶ Recognition of a man of God.

4 Keys To The Holy Spirit Life

1.   *Read The Word Of God.* Nothing is more important than this powerful success habit. "Now ye are clean through the word which I have spoken unto you" (John 15:3).

> ▶ *Jesus unveiled the mystery of joy in His teaching:* "These things have I spoken unto you, that My joy might remain in you, and that your joy might be full" (John 15:11).

Your happiest days will be those days that you are *speaking* His Word to others, *memorizing* His Word, *reading* His Word, *listening* to His Word on cassette and *singing* His Word.

Everything you have always wanted is within His Word. *Everything.* Everything created was produced when He *spoke.* When He desired something—He spoke.

▶ His Word creates inner peace.
▶ His Word creates a climate of comfort.
▶ His Word warns of pitfalls.
▶ His Word purifies your mind.
▶ His Word changes your very nature.

2.   *Keep Your Daily Appointment In The Secret Place, Your Place Of Prayer.* David had such a place. "One thing have I desired of the Lord, that will I seek after; that I may dwell in the house of the Lord all the days of my life, to behold the beauty of the Lord, and to inquire in His temple." (Psalm 27:4).

▶ *Begin each day* in the Secret Place expecting Him to speak to you.

▶ *Stay long enough* to create a memory. You will only return to a Place of Pleasure.

3. *Sing To The Holy Spirit Continually.* "...come before His presence with singing" (Psalm 100:2). Keep music playing throughout your home and in the Secret Place.

4. *Use Your Personal Prayer Language When You Pray.* It is the most neglected weapon in the body of Christ today. "For he that speaketh in an unknown tongue speaketh not unto men, but unto God: for no man understandeth him;" (1 Corinthians 14:2).

The Holy Spirit is your only true Source, the Master Source for *One Thousand Times More.*

RECOMMENDED BOOKS AND TAPES:

B-23	Seeds Of Wisdom On Prayer (32 Page Book/$3)
B-26	The God Book (157 Page Book/$10)
B-27	The Jesus Book (164 Page Book/$10)
B-78	The Mentor's Manna On The Secret Place (52 Page Book/$3)
B-80	The Greatest Success Habit on Earth (32 Page Book/$3)
B-100	The Holy Spirit Handbook (Book/$10)
SB-02	Secret Place Songbook (Songbook/$15)
TS-37	The Greatest Secret Of The Universe (Six Tapes/$30)
TS-59	Songs From The Secret Place (Six Music Tapes/$30)
TSB-100	The Holy Spirit Handbook (Six Tapes/$30)

❧ 2 ❧

DEFINE THE UNCOMMON DREAM THAT ENERGIZES YOU.

Your Dream Is The Invisible Picture Within You.

The Holy Spirit begins everything with an invisible picture within you. *Everything.*

I am not referring to the fragments of thought you experience after eating a pizza or late night meal! I am talking about the invisible *desire* of something you want to become, do or have.

48 Facts About Your Uncommon Dream

1. *The Uncommon Dream Is Anything You Want To Become, Do Or Have During Your Life On Earth.* What do you Dream of becoming? Doing? Possessing? Do not let go of it. You are in the picture, The Real You.

Let me give you an example. You may say, "Well, I would love to own a beautiful yacht." Really? Or, do you actually see yourself standing on that yacht, sailing along under a beautiful sky? Of course you do. You do not want to simply own a yacht, sitting quietly in the water at the harbor. You are seeing *yourself* standing on that yacht, in the midst of your friends with ice tea in one hand, and a smile on your face. You are seeing The Real You—*You-In-The-Future.*

2. *The Uncommon Dream Is The Real You In Your Future, Rather Than Your Present.* The Real You is not flawed, weak and confused. The Real You is the you matured, developed and imprinted with the plan of God. God keeps looking at The Real You, The *You-In-The-Future.*

Something is keeping God excited about you. He is staying connected with you through every season—for a reason. Find out what it is!

3. *An Uncommon Dream Must Be Believed And Pursued.* Joseph chose to embrace the Dream. He fed it. He nurtured it.

4. *The Uncommon Dream Is Your Personal Responsibility To Feed And Grow.* At some point in your life, God will *Imprint* you. He will brand you, like a rancher brands a young calf. He will place in you a picture so strong that you almost lose your breath. It fills up your Thought World, abruptly shoving every other Thought out of the way. You become consumed. Nothing else matters—but that Dream. It is a picture that God Himself has seen, *You-In-The-Future.*

You can believe it or doubt it.

You must feed it or starve it.

You can strengthen or weaken it.

You can grow it or ignore it.

Through your *words.* Through *relationships.* Through your Daily Success Routine.

5. *Satan Uses Pictures Of Your Past To Blur And Distort The Picture Of Your Future, The Uncommon Dream.* Judas could not shake the picture of his past, because he had ignored the revelation of Jesus concerning his future.

6. *When You Ignore The Word Of A Prophet Regarding Your Future, The Uncommon Dream Can Weaken And Die Within You.* You can die the death of a suicide, like Judas. Or, you can die the death of Saul, who failed to value the Uncommon Dream birthed in others.

7. *Your Family Will Often Focus On Your Weaknesses Instead Of The Uncommon Dream Within You.* So, you become preoccupied with correcting your flaws, instead of marketing your strengths. When you look in the mirror, you look for things to correct, instead of what to *enjoy.* Eventually, you begin to build your life and your day around your weakness.

Yesterday is not in your future. God does not intend for it to appear again in your life. "Forgetting those things which are behind, and reaching forth unto those things which are before," Paul advised. "Remember ye not the former things, neither consider the things of old. Behold, I will do a new thing; now it shall spring forth;" (Isaiah 43:18,19).

You must unclutter your mind.

You must unclutter your life.

You must unclutter your conversations.

8. *You Must Keep Speaking The Picture God Keeps Seeing.* Abraham determined his greatest Dream. God showed him a picture of the stars and

the sand of the sea and said that is what his children would be like.

"Abraham, you are going to be the most uncommon father on the earth."

"Me? You've got to be kidding, God!"

God wanted Abraham to *think* about the Dream, talk about the Dream, *tell* others about the Dream. Think, Talk and Tell.

9. *Your Conduct Is Being Decided By The Uncommon Dream You Are Believing—The Real You-In-The-Future.*

10. *Your Daily Conversation Is A Reflection Of The Uncommon Dream You Are Seeing.* The Real *You-In-The-Future.* Stop feeding and replaying old pictures of disappointments.

11. *Your Future Cannot Begin Until You Start Feeding The Uncommon Dream Within You.* You are stopping it from occurring.

12. *God Is Committed To The Uncommon Dream, Whether You See It Or Not.* Peter is an example. He was continually making mistakes. Yet, Jesus said, "Simon, Simon, behold, satan hath desired to have you, that he may sift you as wheat: But I have prayed for thee, that thy faith fail not: and when thou art converted, strengthen thy brethren" (Luke 22:31,32).

13. *Weak Men Become Strong Men When Their Internal Picture, The Uncommon Dream, Changes.* Jesus knew Peter would change when his Internal Picture, The Uncommon Dream changed. Jesus saw Peter as the incredible preacher, not the One Who Denied Him (Luke 22:31,32).

14. *God Uses An Uncommon Dream To Birth*

Hope. The story of Joseph is fascinating. (Read it in the book of Genesis.) He had a Dream during the night that affected him in a dramatic way. He saw a picture (of himself) in *authority.* Others were bowing down to him. It was the opposite of his present life experience. His brothers hated him. He was under their rule and dominion. He was the family errand boy. But, God used a picture to stir his hope that the present would end and a change would occur.

15. *Any Announcement Of The Uncommon Dream Within You Will Agitate Your Enemies.* You see, your Dream intimidates those lacking your boldness. Doubters are agitated by your faith and confidence. They feel inferior to it. So, when you discuss The Uncommon Dream of your life, expect someone to become an adversary or a doubter.

16. *Every Appointment You Make Should Be A Stepping Stone Toward The Fulfillment Of The Uncommon Dream.* Do not waste your time with distractions. Unclutter your life by uncluttering your day.

17. *If You Neglect The Uncommon Dream Within You, It Will Eventually Wither And Die.* Anything living requires food. The Dream within you is a vibrant, living picture of the future *You-In-The-Future...*and requires nurturing, confidence, faith and energy.

18. *The Uncommon Dream Will Accompany You On Every Journey Through Life, Even When Your Best Friends Do Not Have The Time.* That is the power of your Dream. It is the Invisible Escort, the Constant Companion, Daily Advisor.

19. *The Uncommon Dream Will Birth Changes In Your Relationships.* Those who admire The Dream will want to participate and become involved. Those who are intimidated by The *Uncommon Dream* may withdraw. Relationships will always move and shift proportionate to your passion for your Dream.

20. *The Uncommon Dream Will Always Influence What You Do First Each Morning.* When Mohammed Ali determined to become the heavyweight champion of the world, his routine changed. He began to awaken early each morning for road work. When the late Mary Kay Ash determined to have her incredible business, she created a plan every single morning of the six most important things she would do that day. What you do first every morning is an indication of what you consider the most valuable and important thing you can do with your life.

21. *The Uncommon Dream Can Begin With Whatever Is In Your Heart Today.* What do you feel strongly about right now? What stays on your mind the most throughout the day?

22. *The Uncommon Dream Can Come True Regardless Of Your Personal Limitations.* Stop evaluating your handicaps. Look for the reasons you can succeed. Do not inventory your needs. Inventory your *Seeds*—that which you have been given by God.

23. *The Uncommon Dream Can Only Be Birthed Through Uncommon Faith.* Feed your faith by reading the biographies and experiences of uncommon men. Greatness is everywhere around

you, *merely awaiting your recognition of it.* When you listen to the vocabulary of achievers, your faith will leap. In Scriptures, it is very clear that "faith comes by hearing"—hearing the Word of God.

24. *The Uncommon Dream Deserves The Highest Standard Of Excellence Possible.* Develop a passion for details. Do everything you do at the highest level of quality and excellence you presently can.

25. *The Uncommon Dream Determines Who Will Pursue And Reach For You.* If your Dream is to have the most efficient housecleaning crew and company in the state, those who need that service will find you. You see, your Dream is a magnet for those whose problems can be solved by you.

26. *The Uncommon Dream Is Born Within You, Not Borrowed From Another.* Follow the passion within you. Everyone has an opinion of what you ought to do with your life, but you alone can know whether it is a Dream birthed within yourself.

27. *The Uncommon Dream Is Often Birthed From Uncommon Pain And Painful Memories.* Those raised in poverty often have a passion for blessing and prosperity. Those who had childhood sickness, often live their life helping others develop uncommon health.

28. *The Uncommon Dream Within You Is Often Misunderstood By Those Closest To You.* Joseph experienced this in that powerful story of Biblical times. His brothers hated The Dream that excited him. *Your family is a test or a reward.* Everything you may face in your future is already

in your home. A Judas? Doubting Thomas? God gives you an environment to expose your limitations, correct your flaws and develop a life plan in the presence of those who really love you, before you reach the enemy battle ground.

29. *The Uncommon Dream Is Your Companion, Moving You Steadily Away From Your Present And Into Your Future.* Without that invisible and powerful picture within you, the present will become permanent. You must have a picture of tomorrow.

30. *The Uncommon Dream Is Your Significant Difference From Others.* Others may not understand it. That invisible wall is merely another reminder that The Dream is different from others.

31. *The Uncommon Dream May Be So Big That It Makes You Feel Fearful, Inadequate Or Inferior.* When Moses received the instructions from God that he was a deliverer, fear struck. He did not feel capable. That is why God becomes more necessary every day in your life.

32. *The Uncommon Dream May Require A Geographical Change.* Ruth had to leave Moab. Abraham had to leave his kinfolks. Joseph left his home and ended up in Egypt. Geography determines what grows within you, your weakness or your strength. Geography determines the *favor* that comes toward you. You must be *seen* before you can be promoted.

33. *The Uncommon Dream May Require More Finances Than You Presently Possess Or Have Ever Imagined.* Late one night, the late Dr. Lester

Sumrall and I were talking. He told me, "Every time God told me to do something great, I didn't have any money to do it. He just told me do it, so I started doing it." That requires total addiction to obedience.

34. *The Uncommon Dream Can Become So Strong That It Burns Within You With Or Without The Encouragement Of Others.* Joseph had no one to encourage him toward his Dream. David received no encouragement from his brothers in facing Goliath. As you remain in the presence of the Holy Spirit, the picture of tomorrow will burn brighter and greater. It can continue, whether others help you or not!

35. *The Uncommon Dream Must Be Desirable Enough To Qualify For Your Total Focus.* You will only succeed with an obsession. When God births The Dream, it will require *all* of you.

36. *The Uncommon Dream Qualifies Those Who Deserve Access To You.* Many will reach. You must screen the pursuers. Jesus experienced this and once said, "Who is My mother? and who are My brethren?" He was not distancing Himself from His family. He was *qualifying* those who deserved access to Him. He never went home with Pharisees, yet had an entire meal with Zacchaeus, the tax collector.

37. *The Uncommon Dream Within You Will Burst Uncommon Passion That Dominates Every Conversation You Enter.* Talk only about the things that matter in life. When God births a vision, it will dominate every conversation. Many years ago, I spent several days with Mark Buntain in

Calcutta, India. The whole world knew Mark Buntain. Continuously, he would burst into his passionate praying and discussion of Calcutta. While shopping one day, he burst into a great description of his passion for Calcutta. Why? The Uncommon Dream and vision will be too much to contain.

38. *The Uncommon Dream Will Eliminate Wrong People From Your Life.* When you insist on that which is right, wrong people will find you unbearable.

39. *The Uncommon Dream Will Attract Uncommon Opposition.* Everything good has an enemy. Expect it. *Prepare* for it.

40. *The Uncommon Dream Will Often Magnify The Undesirable Traits Of Your Present Circumstances.* When your vision is tomorrow, your present seems intolerable. Be careful about developing unthankfulness and ingratitude. It is difficult to walk between two worlds—today and tomorrow.

41. *The Uncommon Dream Will Only Succeed Proportionate To Your Service To Others.* Joseph had to serve Potiphar well before he qualified for Pharaoh. Ruth ministered to Naomi, before achieving the level of excellence to qualify for Boaz. Esther pleased the king long before she began to ask for special favor.

42. *The Uncommon Dream Will Require Uncommon Favor.* Sow it. Decree it. Expect it.

43. *The Uncommon Dream Will Require Total Focus.* The Only Reason Men Fail Is Broken Focus. Focus determines persistence. Focus generates *energy*. You will be remembered in life for

your focus.

44. *The Uncommon Dream Will Require Uncommon Preparation.* David began preparing for the great temple of Jerusalem long before Solomon finished it or even started it! Jesus took 30 years preparing for three and a half years of ministry.

45. *Any Disrespect You Show Others Can Set Your Dream Back For Many Years.* As God prepared Moses for leadership, he got involved with the murder of an Egyptian. It cost him years.

46. *When You Boldly Announce Your Dream, You Will Create An Instant Bond With Every Person Who Wanted To Accomplish The Same Dream.* Many have seen their Dreams dashed on the Rocks of Disappointment. When they observe your success, hope leaps again within them. They want to be bonded with someone who is persistent to do it.

47. *Respect For Every Relationship Connected To The Uncommon Dream Will Guarantee Its Fulfillment.* Treasure them. Protect them. Recognize those God has placed close to you. *They are Golden Gates to One Thousand Times More.*

48. *Uncommon Achievers Visualize Their Dream Continuously.* Place pictures on the wall of where you want to travel. Keep a photograph of the new house you desire on the bulletin board. Talk it. Think it. *Define* it. *Refine* it. *Confine* your focus to it. Remember that your mind *replays* the past; your imagination pre-plays the future. David visualized past triumphs that energized him before he faced Goliath. Then, he declared his intention that Goliath's head would be severed.

What Happens In Your Mind Often Happens In Time. You must visualize increase. You must talk about increase. You must move every hour in your life toward increase. The Promise of *One Thousand Times More* goes to those daring to Dream, plan and visualize supernatural increase.

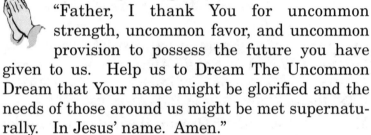

Our Prayer Together...

"Father, I thank You for uncommon strength, uncommon favor, and uncommon provision to possess the future you have given to us. Help us to Dream The Uncommon Dream that Your name might be glorified and the needs of those around us might be met supernaturally. In Jesus' name. Amen."

RECOMMENDED BOOKS AND TAPES:

B-11	Dream Seeds (112 Page Book/$9)
B-13	Seeds of Wisdom On Dreams And Goals (32 Page Book/$3)
B-15	Seeds Of Wisdom on Miracles (32 Page Book/$3)
B-68	The Gift Of Wisdom For Achievers (31 Page Book/$10)
TSB-65	Born To Taste The Grapes (Six Tapes/$30)
TS-14	How To Stay Motivated (Six Tapes/$30)
TS-16	The Double Diamond and The Millionaire Mentality (Six Tapes/$30)
TS-31	The Double Diamond and Dreams, Decisions, Destiny (Six Tapes/$30)
VI-4	7 Ways To Stay Motivated (Video/$25)
VI-5	5 Keys For Achieving Goals (Video/$25)

∽ 3 ∽

DETERMINE TO WHOM YOU HAVE BEEN ASSIGNED.

You Were Created To Solve A Problem.

Find out what it is and give yourself to excellence. You see, everything created is a solution to an existing problem. Eyes see. Ears hear. Hands reach. Feet walk. Your mouth speaks. Mechanics solve car problems. Lawyers solve legal problems. Mothers solve emotional problems.

Your Assignment is any problem God has qualified or provided a passion for you to solve.

Here Are 12 Facts You Must Know And Recognize About Your Assignment

1. *Your Assignment Is Decided By God And Discovered By You.* The automobile did not decide that it would be an automobile. Henry Ford did. The airplane did not determine to be an airplane. The Wright brothers did.

The Creator decides.

The creation discovers.

2. *Your Assignment Was Decided By The Holy Spirit, Even While You Were In The Womb Of*

Your Mother. Jeremiah experienced this (read Jeremiah 1:5-8). The Holy Spirit, Who created you, has decided your Assignment on the earth.

3. *Your Assignment Is Always To A Person Or A People.* Moses' Assignment was to the Israelites. Aaron's Assignment was to Moses. How do you discern to whom you have been sent? Ask yourself truthful questions. Whose *failure* would bring you tears? Whose *success* stays on your mind all the time? Whose pain do you feel when you enter their presence? Whose achievements bring excitement to you?

4. *Your Assignment Is Geographical.* The Assignment of Ruth took her to Bethlehem. The Assignment of Joseph brought him to Egypt. The Assignment of Jesus brought Him to the cross. You belong somewhere. Somebody is waiting for you there.

> ▶ When You Are Where You Have Been Assigned, The Right People Will See You.
> ▶ When The Right People See You, Favor Flows.
> ▶ Where You Are Matters As Much As What You Are.
> ▶ Where You Are Will Determine What Grows Within You, Weeds Or Flowers, Weaknesses Or Strengths.

5. *Your Assignment Determines What Is Important To You.* The hair stylist notices hair. The tailor notices clothes.

6. *What You Love The Most Is A Clue To Your Assignment.* If you love computers, that is where your Wisdom lies. If you love children, you

will have Wisdom toward children. These are clues to your passion.

7. *What Angers You Is A Clue To Something You Are Assigned To Correct.* When Moses saw an Egyptian beating up an Israelite, anger came. Why? He was a deliverer.

8. *What Saddens You Is A Clue To Something You Are Assigned To Heal.* Something brings you pain. What is it? That is a clue to something God is qualifying you to mend.

9. *Your Assignment Will Require Seasons Of Preparation.* You will experience seasons of insignificance, disillusionment, disappointment, mentorship, possibly restoration.

10. *Your Assignment Determines Who Will Celebrate You.* When your teeth hurt, you really will "celebrate" the dentist! When your hair grows too long, you "celebrate" the hair stylist. So, somebody is reaching for you today. That is a clue to your Assignment.

11. *Your Provision Is Only Guaranteed At The Place Of Your Assignment, The Place Of Obedience.* Elijah was instructed to go to the brook. When he obeyed, the raven showed up with his meal. One day the raven did not return. The brook dried up. Why? His Assignment had *changed.* God had instructed him to go to Zarephath, the village of a starving widow. When he went to her house as an act of obedience, God provided miraculously throughout the famine *there.* John Olsteen, my widely respected friend, always says—"You must find your own place called 'There.' That is where God's provision will be."

12. *Your Assignment Is Always To Solve A Problem.* What problems do you *notice?* What problems do you *think* about the most? What problems are you the *most passionate* about solving around you?

Here Are 8 Facts You Should Always Remember About Problem Solving

1. *You Are Not Assigned To Solve Problems For Everybody.* Jesus Himself stated that He did not come to those who were whole, but to those who were sick. He never went home with Pharisees. He went home with those who perceived His value.

You *cannot* solve every kind of problem you experience or see. Jesus *left* earth, while it was *still* filled with problems. Jesus never felt responsible for solving *every* problem He saw. Even those who were blind were required to call upon Him if they desired healing. The woman with an issue of blood had to persist in crawling through the crowd to touch the hem of His garment—before she was healed. Jesus never felt responsible for solving every problem He was capable of solving.

2. *You Will Only Be Remembered For The Problems You Solve Or The Ones You Create.* Billy Graham will be remembered for the spiritual problems he solved. Hitler will be remembered for the atrocious crimes he committed and the problems he birthed.

3. *Your Rewards In Life Will Be Determined By The Problems You Are Willing To Solve For Others.* A garbage collector may receive $15 an

hour while a lawyer receives $200 an hour. Why? The problems they have chosen to solve determines the salary they will receive.

4. *When You Solve A Problem Better Than Anyone Else, You Will Be Pursued And Rewarded.* There is a reason I drive further to get a haircut than the closest hair salon. The lady who cuts my hair is the best.

5. *When You Solve A Problem Quicker Than Anyone Else, You Will Be Rewarded Proportionately.* A small print shop close to my house is quite successful. Their prices are high. Why do people go? They do the work *immediately* instead of waiting.

6. *When You Solve A Problem With A Cheerful Attitude, Your Boss Will Note It And Usually Reward You For It.* Attitude is important to CEO's in the corporate world.

7. *Your Willingness To Solve A Problem At Any Time Can Affect Your Salary And Respect In The Local Community.* I have seen small cafes stay open for years without having food of the highest quality. Why? They stayed open *24 hours.*

8. *Excel In Your Present Assignment And The News Will Travel.* When Boaz, the wealthy landowner, noticed Ruth, he discussed her with the servants. They knew who she was. They knew when she worked and when she did not. They knew that she was personally a servant to Naomi, her mother-in-law. Her uncommon goodness was recognized by an uncommon achiever. The rest is history. She gave birth to the lineage of David, Solomon and Jesus.

The Greatest Success Law I Have Ever Discovered!

What You Make Happen For Others, God Will Make Happen For You. God spoke this sentence to me on my fifth day of a personal fast in Houston, Texas, many years ago. It changed me forever. I learned that when I concentrated on the success of *others,* God would concentrate on my own success. Remember Job? When he prayed for his friends, that is when God turned his own captivity.

Checklist For Excellence

1. What do you *love* to do the most each day?

2. *To whom* have you been assigned for the present season?

3. Is your present performance the *highest* and ultimate level of excellence you could possibly do?

4. What are you doing that is cluttering your life each day?

5. Who is assigned to you?

6. Is your present season a *test* or a *reward?*

7. Whose pain truly affects your heart?

8. Whose joy do you long to see?

Recognizing your own Assignment is a Golden Key in unlocking the waves of blessing—for the *One Thousand Times More* God promised into your life.

Our Prayer Together...
"Holy Spirit, You have determined my Assignment. Show me where I belong. Bring me swiftly to those to whom I have been assigned. I can make a difference in their life. Give me the patience to endure any season of isolation or frustration I am experiencing. Your plan is my goal and obsession. In Jesus' name. Amen."

RECOMMENDED BOOKS AND TAPES:

B-07	Battle Techniques For War Weary Saints (32 Page Book/$3)
B-74	The Assignment: The Dream And The Destiny, Vol. 1 (151 Page Book/$10)
B-75	The Assignment: The Anointing And The Adversity, Vol. 2 (143 Page Book/$10)
MML-05	The Mentor's Manna Library On The Assignment #4 (Two Tapes And A Book/$10)
TS-5	How To Walk Through Fire (Six Tapes/$30)
TS-23	31 Secrets Of The Uncommon Problem Solver (Six Tapes/$30)
TS-29	The Double Diamond and Gifts, Goals and Guts (Six Tapes/$30)
VI-10	Getting Things Done (Video/$25)

If You Want To
Experience The Mantle Of
One Thousand Times More,
You Must Celebrate The
Mantle Of The Intercessor
God Has Assigned
To Your Life.

-MIKE MURDOCK

INVEST IN UNCOMMON MENTORSHIP.

Mentorship Is The Transference Of Wisdom.

Wisdom is the most powerful force on earth. It is the difference between poverty and prosperity; decrease and increase; loss and gain. Throughout the Ancient Writings comes the teaching, "Wisdom is the principal thing;" (Proverbs 4:7).

Here Are 12 Important Facts You Should Know About Wisdom

1. *Wisdom Is The Master Key To Releasing All The Treasures Of Life Contained In God's Promise Of One Thousand Times More.* Solomon discovered this. In his unforgettable Dream, God spoke, "Because this was in thine heart, and thou hast not asked riches, wealth, or honour, nor the life of thine enemies, neither yet hast asked long life; but hast asked wisdom and knowledge for thyself, that thou mayest judge My people, over whom I have made thee king: Wisdom and knowledge is granted unto thee; and I will give thee riches, and wealth, and honour, such as none of the kings have had that have been before thee, neither shall there any after thee have the like" (2 Chronicles 1:11,12).

2. *Wisdom Is Not Necessarily Inherited Genetically Through Your Bloodline.* A wise father

can have a foolish son. "A wise son maketh a glad father: but a foolish son is the heaviness of his mother" (Proverbs 10:1; see also Proverbs 10:5).

3. *All The Treasures Of Wisdom And Knowledge Are Hidden In Jesus Christ.* "That their hearts might be comforted, being knit together in love, and unto all riches of the full assurance of understanding, to the acknowledgment of the mystery of God, and of the Father, and of Christ; In Whom are hid all the treasures of wisdom and knowledge" (Colossians 2:2,3).

Everything you could possibly desire, including *One Thousand Times More,* will come through your obedience and relationship with Jesus Christ!

4. *The Holy Spirit Is The Spirit Of Wisdom That Imparts And Uses Your Gifts, Talents And Skills.* "...every wisehearted man, in whom the Lord put wisdom and understanding to know how to work all manner of work for the service of the sanctuary, according to all that the Lord had commanded" (Exodus 36:1; see also 1 Corinthians 12).

5. *Wisdom Is More Powerful Than Weapons Of War.* "Wisdom is better than weapons of war:" (Ecclesiastes 9:18).

6. *The Mantle Of Wisdom Can Make You Ten Times Stronger Than Those Without It.* "Wisdom strengtheneth the wise more than ten mighty men which are in the city" (Ecclesiastes 7:19).

7. *Wisdom Makes Your Enemies Helpless Against You.* "For I will give you a mouth and wisdom, which all your adversaries shall not be able to gainsay nor resist" (Luke 21:15).

8. *Wisdom Creates Currents Of Favor And Recognition Toward You.* "Exalt her, and she shall promote thee: she shall bring thee to honour, when thou dost embrace her" (Proverbs 4:8). One Thousand Times More Wisdom will create One Thousand Times More favor toward your life!

9. *Wisdom Guarantees Your Promotion.* "Exalt her, and she shall promote thee: she shall bring thee to honour, when thou dost embrace her. She shall give to thine head an ornament of grace: a crown of glory shall she deliver to thee" (Proverbs 4:8,9).

10. *When You Increase Your Wisdom, You Will Increase Your Wealth.* "Riches and honour are with Me; yea, durable riches and righteousness" (Proverbs 8:18).

11. *Your Investment In Books And Tapes Is Proof Of Your Passion For Wisdom.* Paul urged Timothy, "Study to shew thyself approved" (2 Timothy 2:15). Your willingness to invest in knowledge is a signal that you understand the rewards of Wisdom.

12. *Wisdom Is Transferred Through Relationship.* "He that walketh with wise men shall be wise: but a companion of fools shall be destroyed" (Proverbs 13:20).

Yes, Wisdom can even be imparted by the laying on of hands of a powerful man of God. "And Joshua the son of Nun was full of the spirit of wisdom; for Moses had laid his hands upon him: and the children of Israel hearkened unto him," (Deuteronomy 34:9). Wisdom even affects the willingness of others to listen to you!

There are two ways to receive Wisdom throughout your life: *mistakes and Mentors.*

Mentors are *gifts* from God.

Mentors are *gates* to greatness.

Mentors are *bridges* to blessings.

Mentors create uncommon *increase.*

Mentors are more than just teachers. Teachers focus on information while a Mentor focuses on the protégé.

An Uncommon Mentor is more than a cheer-leader. He is a coach, showing you how to achieve your goal.

There Are 4 Types Of Mentorship

1. *Parental Mentorship Is The Wisdom Received Through Your Parents.* It is the first proof of humility. It involves the first commandment with a promise that if you honor your mother and father, it will go well with you throughout your life-time (see Ephesians 6:1-3).

2. *Pastoral Mentorship Is The Wisdom Received Through Your Spiritual Leader And Pastor Of Your Church.* Scripture commands us to: "Not forsaking the assembling of ourselves togeth-er,...and so much the more, as ye see the day approaching" (Hebrews 10:25).

3. *Professional Mentorship Is The Wisdom You Receive Through Your Employer, Supervisors And Career Sages* (read Ephesians 6:4-8).

4. *Prophetic Mentorship Is Wisdom That Comes Through Uncommon Anointings Of Uncommon Men Of God Assigned To You During*

Crisis And Critical Turning Points Of Your Life. It may be healing, financial or relationship oriented. But, the Ancient Writings confirm that the *secrets of God are hidden inside men and women of God.* "Surely the Lord God will do nothing, but He revealeth His secret unto His servants the prophets" (Amos 3:7).

"Believe in the Lord your God, so shall ye be established; believe His prophets, so shall ye prosper" (2 Chronicles 20:20). God reveals information to those who walk in obedience to Him. When you honor their mantle, extraordinary promotion and events occur. One of the most powerful examples I have ever studied was in the life of Saul, son of Kish. Saul discovered this kind of impartation when he and his servant pursued the presence of Samuel, the prophet. Within hours, Saul was anointed for kingship. It happened in a single day. Why? He entered the presence of an uncommon man of God who could see into his future.

Never forget this powerful principle: "The Secret of the Lord is with them that fear Him; and He will shew them His covenant" (Psalm 25:14).

13 Important Facts About Uncommon Mentorship

1. *Uncommon Mentorship Will Require The Investment Of Time.* Elisha stayed in the presence of Elijah. Ruth persisted in remaining with Naomi even though she had to move into another country. Joshua stayed under the authority of Moses. David always pursued the presence and counsel of

Samuel, his prophet and Mentor. The disciples invested time in the presence of Jesus, away from the crowds.

2. *Everything You Know Came Through Mentorship.* When you were a baby, you were taught to walk, eat and even dress yourself.

3. *Uncommon Mentors Can Create Uncommon Protégés.* Look at the fishermen, Peter, James and John, who became renown. They simply had an Uncommon Mentor. An Uncommon Mentor can completely erase the scars and defects created by past prejudices and wounds. Jesus did it for the 12 disciples. The Holy Spirit is doing it for many today.

4. *Uncommon Mentors Require Pursuit.* You always reach for what you truly desire. The passion within you will determine your pursuit of your Mentor.

5. *An Uncommon Dream Will Always Require Uncommon Mentorship.* Solomon received a powerful Assignment to build the great temple of Jerusalem. His Mentor? The incredible and unforgettable King David. He even helped him collect the materials necessary for its completion.

6. *Uncommon Mentorship Can Take Place Anywhere.* Jesus taught in synagogues (Luke 13:10). Then, He also taught in villages (Mark 6:6).

7. *The Uncommon Mentor Will Always Be An Enemy To The Enemy Of His Protégé.* Jesus reflected this when He warned Peter regarding satan. "Simon, Simon, behold, satan hath desired to have you, that he may sift you as wheat: But I have prayed for thee, that thy faith fail not: and

when thou art converted, strengthen thy brethren" (Luke 22:31,32). The Mentor will fight against any philosophy, pitfalls or prejudices that would rob the protégé of experiencing the *One Thousand Times More* Blessing in his life.

8. *The Uncommon Mentor Knows Precisely The Path The Protégé Must Take To Unleash The Harvest Of One Thousand Times More.* That is why Paul advised Timothy to "shew himself approved unto God, a workman that needeth not to be ashamed."

9. *The Uncommon Mentor Willingly Risks The Anger And Even The Alienation Of Protégés To Keep Them Qualified To Receive The Increase Of One Thousand Times More.* You see, the focus of the Mentor is the protection of the protégé, not the love from the protégé. The Prophet Samuel was swift to correct Saul and David. Why? To prevent their experience of pain.

10. *The Uncommon Mentor Has Something You Do Not Have Because He Knows Something You Do Not Know.* Discoveries determine progress. Discoveries determine relationships. "Wisdom is the principal thing; Exalt her, and she shall promote thee: she shall bring thee to honour, when thou dost embrace her" (Proverbs 4:7,8).

11. *The Uncommon Mentor Measures The Passion Of The Protégé By His Pursuit Of The Mentor.* What You Respect, You Will Attract. You will never possess what you are unwilling to pursue.

12. *The Uncommon Mentor Exposes Fraudulent People To His Protégé.* Jesus exposed

the Pharisees to His disciples, "But all their works they do for to be seen of men: they make broad their phylacteries, and enlarge the borders of their garments," (Matthew 23:5). One of the master keys to unlocking *One Thousand Times More* in your life is to detect enemies and thieves of increase in your life. That is one of the powerful benefits of staying close to a proven and Uncommon Mentor.

13. *The Uncommon Mentor Can Often Predict The Potential Weakness And Pitfalls Of A Protégé.* Jesus did this for Peter. "I tell thee, Peter, the cock shall not crow this day, before that thou shalt thrice deny that thou knowest Me" (Luke 22:34). Now, the Mentor does not withdraw from the protégé because of it. He becomes an *intercessor* because of it (read Luke 22:31,32)!

I am just now learning how to be a protégé after all these years of life and ministry. Here are some of the things that I am learning.

The 4 Kinds Of Protégés

1. *The Passive Protégé.* They observe. They listen. But, they only reach when it is convenient for them. They are slow to ask sincere and probing questions. They want the Mentor to become aggressive, make all the suggestions and stop them from floundering or crashing. They want the Mentor to be more committed to their success then they are willing to commit themselves. They only read a book if the Mentor insists on it. Then, they would rather you purchase it for them! They interpret the aggressiveness of a Mentor as proof of his love. They sincerely feel that the Mentor is respon-

sible for pursuing them and imparting to them. Passive protégés usually fail or become embittered.

2. *The Parasite Protégé.* They want your *influence,* not your correction. They stay close for the network of relationships involved. Name droppers, they will use your name strategically with other people to show relationship. They want the *profit* from relationship without the *cost* of discipleship. They want what the Mentor has earned, not what he has learned. They ride the reputation of a Mentor without the seasons of preparation required.

3. *The Productive Protégé.* He recognized the achievements of the Mentor. He possesses a servant's heart. He refuses to make a major decision without the counsel and feedback of his Mentor. He considers the Uncommon Mentor to be a dominant gift from God for accelerating his own ministry and life. The Productive Protégé truly loves his Mentor, wants to experience his Mentor and feel his heart. The Apostle Paul wrote, "And we beseech you, brethren, to know them which labour among you, and are over you in the Lord, and admonish you; And to esteem them very highly in love for their work's sake" (1 Thessalonians 5:12,13).

4. *The Prodigal Protégé.* They move toward popularity. They are fad conscious. They fall into the comparison trap, between what their Mentor offers them and someone else offers them. They are obviously "for hire." They will move away from a Mentor the moment there is serious correction, a higher salary offered, or when the Mentor experi-

ences an unexpected disaster. Just like the prodigal son wanted what the father had for his own
pleasure, so it is with the prodigal protégé.

13 Qualities Of An Uncommon Protégé

1. *The Uncommon Protégé Will Invest
Whatever Is Necessary To Stay In The Presence Of
An Uncommon Mentor.* Ruth persisted in following
Naomi to Bethlehem. "Intreat me not to leave
thee, or to return from following after thee: for
whither thou goest, I will go;" (Ruth 1:16).

2. *The Uncommon Protégé Will Embrace
The Counsel Of The Mentor.* God takes it seriously.
In fact, during the days of Moses, the rebellious
protégé was always punished. "And the man that
will do presumptuously, and will not hearken unto
the priest that standeth to minister there before
the Lord thy God, or unto the judge, even that man
shall die: and thou shalt put away the evil from
Israel. And all the people shall hear, and fear, and
do no more presumptuously" (Deuteronomy
17:12,13).

3. *The Uncommon Protégé Will Ultimately
Receive The Mantle Of The Mentor He Most
Respects.* The transference of the anointing is not
a fantasy. It is a fact. The Apostle Paul wrote,
"Wherefore I put thee in remembrance that thou
stir up the gift of God, which is in thee by the put-
ting on of *my* hands" (2 Timothy 1:6).

Joshua experienced it, "There shall not any
man be able to stand before thee all the days of thy
life: as I was with Moses, so I will be with thee: I
will not fail thee, nor forsake thee" (Joshua 1:5).

Saul experienced it through Samuel. Saul and his servant brought an offering to Samuel and the anointing began to flow. Samuel anointed him for kingship. (Read 1 Samuel 9 and 10 for a remarkable understanding of the transference of the anointing.)

You will never receive an anointing for *One Thousand Times More* from someone who is anti-prosperity, anti-healing and critical of every man of God who preaches faith. You must pursue the mantle of those who possess what you desire.

4. *The Uncommon Protégé Treasures The Mantle Of Intercessors Assigned To Him.* The Israelites said to the Prophet Samuel, "Pray for thy servants unto the Lord thy God, that we die not: for we have added unto all our sins this evil, to ask us a king" (1 Samuel 12:19).

Seven weeks ago, a prosperous couple spread their financial sheets before me on a table at a church. They pointed to the specific day they had planted a special *Seed* of $58 into my ministry, and they had given me their personal business card. I had agreed to take their business card to my Secret Place and pray for their business. Within 58 days, their business leaped from $200,000 to over one million dollars. Within 58 days! To me, it was not a mystery. They believed in my intercession for them. They believed God wanted them to prosper and have *One Thousand Times More.*

Every month I write a personal letter to thousands of my partners. With the letter, I always enclose a special "Secret Place Faith Agreement Page" where the partners can document their Dreams and desires. Many *ignore* the Faith

Agreement Page. I can ask thousands to send me personal photographs of their family, or a business card to pray for their business. They ignore it, letter after letter. Am I puzzled by their poverty and losses? Not at all. It is not a mystery to me. They simply have not yet recognized the Golden Link to their miracle, the Intercessor.

5. *The Uncommon Protégé Loves To Sow Uncommon Seeds Of Appreciation Into The Life Of His Mentor.* The Queen of Sheba understood this Law of Increase. You must sow into the soil that is greater. She brought gifts (worth over four million dollars!) when she met Solomon for an appointment. "And she came to Jerusalem with a very great train, with camels that bare spices, and very much gold, and precious stones: and when she was come to Solomon, she communed with him of all that was in her heart. And Solomon told her all her questions: there was not any thing hid from the king, which he told her not. And she gave the king an hundred and twenty talents of gold, and of spices very great store, and precious stones: there came no more such abundance of spices as these which the queen of Sheba gave to king Solomon" (1 Kings 10:2,3,10).

Gifts were given to the Master Mentor, the Apostle Paul. "For even in Thessalonica ye sent once and again unto my necessity" (Philippians 4:16). The Apostle Paul believed that gifts *should* be planted into the life of the Mentor. "Thou shalt not muzzle the mouth of the ox that treadeth out the corn...If we have sown unto you spiritual things, is it a great thing if we shall reap your carnal things?" (1 Corinthians 9:9,11).

Any *Seed* you sow into Mentors who have unlocked your faith, your love, and supernatural finances—will come back to you *One Thousand Times More.*

If You Want To Experience The Mantle Of One Thousand Times More, You Must Celebrate The Mantle Of The Intercessor God Has Assigned To Your Life.

6.   *The Uncommon Protégé Clearly Defines And Declares His Expectations Of His Mentor.* Elisha wanted a double portion of the anointing of Elijah. He declared it and received it. What qualifies your Mentor? What does he have or know that you desire? Have you clearly defined to him what you expect?

7.   *The   Uncommon   Protégé   Willingly Discusses His Greatest Dreams With His Mentor.* Ruth expressed her heart to Naomi. Elisha expressed his longing to Elijah. David was swift to declare his eagerness to fight Goliath for King Saul. Vulnerability and openness creates a bond between the Mentor and the Protégé. The Law of Agreement is the foundation for unleashing *One Thousand Times More.*

8.   *The Uncommon Protégé Will Expose His Greatest Fears To His Mentor.* Esther was afraid. She shared her fears with Mordecai. He confronted them and helped her defeat Haman and the cruel strategy to assassinate the Jews. One of the great rewards of the Mentor-Protégé relationship is that "two are better than one." The Mentor provides a climate for considering any idea, any strategy.

9. *The Uncommon Protégé Knows The Powerful Rewards Of Asking.* Mentors answer questions. Answers do not flow from the Mentor until the questions flow to the Mentor.

The Ethiopian eunuch, in Acts 8, was baffled. But, when he *asked* Philip to explain, the miracle started. When you stop asking questions, the answers stop coming. You will never receive the *One Thousand Times More* Harvest without asking the *right* questions.

10. *The Uncommon Protégé Will Discuss His Mistakes And Pain Occurring With His Mentor.* David did this with Samuel. "So David fled, and escaped, and came to Samuel to Ramah, and told him all that Saul had done to him. And he and Samuel went and dwelt in Naioth" (1 Samuel 19:18). The disciples did the same during the great storm (see Matthew 8:24,25).

11. *An Uncommon Protégé Will Publicly Acknowledge And Honor His Mentor.* When I read the lives of uncommon achievers who experience *One Thousand Times More* than those around them, they were protégés of Uncommon Mentors.

Sam Walton gives credit to his father-in-law.

Donald Trump gives credit to his father.

Lee Iacocca gives credit to Robert McNamara.

What is happening in your life? What kind of increases are you presently experiencing? Whose counsel have you been following for the last five years? What questions have you been asking?

12. *An Uncommon Protégé Is Willing To Invest An Uncommon Amount Of Time For Personal Mentorship.* This explained the incredible

success of the Apostle Paul. He pulled aside from a normal schedule and invested three years in Mentorship. "Neither went I up to Jerusalem to them which were apostles before me; but I went into Arabia, and returned again unto Damascus. Then after three years I went up to Jerusalem to see Peter, and abode with him fifteen days" (Galatians 1:17,18).

13. *The Uncommon Protégé Will Invest Whatever It Takes To Unlock His Own Success.*

I will never forget it. After I paid the young store clerk $84 for one small book, my young assistant was stunned.

"I can hardly believe that you paid $84 for one little book!" he exclaimed.

"Oh, son, I didn't. What took this man twenty years to discover, I will now learn within two hours. I'd be a fool not to pay someone $84 to do personal research for me for 24 months!"

Whatever you do, invest in whatever it takes to unleash the next wave of blessing...The Promise of *One Thousand Times More.*

One Thousand Times More.

It is a mystery to millions.

It is a fantasy of millions.

It is a miracle to believers.

But, it is the simple result of following the Laws of Blessing—Uncommon Mentors Always Create Uncommon Protégés.

Invest in Uncommon Mentorship. It is one of the Seven Master Keys to creating *One Thousand Times More* of the Harvest you have long desired in your life.

What You Do Daily
Determines What You
Become Permanently.

-MIKE MURDOCK

～5～

Cultivate The Habit Of Hourly Obedience.

━━━━━━►•◦•◄━━━━━━

Obedience Is The Only Thing God Ever Requires.

It is His obsession. It seems that it is the only thing on His mind. Ever. It is The Master Key to *One Thousand Times More.* "If ye be willing and obedient, ye shall eat the good of the land:" (Isaiah 1:19).

I had a life-changing experience many years ago. God began to reveal to me that my only responsibility was 24 hours of obedience. The past was over. The future was not yet born. My only focus should be 24 hours of *hourly* obedience. Little did I realize that it would launch me into a season of incredible and unexplainable increase in my life. Now, I realize it was the Master Key to *One Thousand Times More.*

The Holy Spirit talked to me about continuous obedience, hour by hour. Previously, I had laughed at novices in the church that always stated, "God told me this, and God told me that." Sadly, because many unlearned and untaught people confuse their imagination with the Holy Spirit, it has been a neglected principle and truth—God *does* talk to you more than anyone else on this earth. *Continuously.*

I was at KJOJ Radio Station in Houston, Texas. My plans were to stay over on Sunday and tape after my Saturday night session. But, I remembered that I had promised the Holy Spirit I would ask Him about *everything.* So, I left the little cubicle and went into the hall where I bowed my head and simply prayed, "Holy Spirit, I would like to remain here and do radio taping tomorrow. Do you want me to do that, or return to Dallas?"

The small inner nudge was to return to Dallas.

"Johnny," I instructed my nephew who was assisting me, "grab your things, we're going to rush to the airport. We have to leave in less than an hour!"

While walking into the plane, the man in front of me suddenly turned.

"Aren't you Mike Murdock?" he asked.

"Yes, I am." I answered.

"Brother, I have been wanting to meet you for many years. I lost my marriage, my home and my business. While going through the worse crisis of my life, somebody sent me your special cassette tapes called, *Grasshopper Complex.* Mike, they changed my life! In fact, today, I am happily married and I make over $30,000 every month in my business. I attribute all of it to your incredible tapes, *The Grasshopper Complex.*" He wrote a check to me for $1,000 as a Seed of Appreciation.

While looking at the check, the inner voice of the Holy Spirit came back to me, "How would you like to be at *the right place at the right time every*

day of your life?" I assured Him that I would...
while looking at the $1,000 check!

A few weeks later, I walked into the Sheraton
Hotel in Washington, DC. It was a National
Religious Broadcasters Convention. As I walked
through, I felt pressured to meet with my staff
inside. One of the television hosts called out and
asked me to do a special interview at that moment.
I replied that I was quite busy and would try to get
back later. As I walked on, it dawned on me that I
had not really asked the Holy Spirit. So, I did,
rather hurriedly.

The inner voice was, "do the interview."

I did. Walking away from the interview down
the hall of the Sheraton Hotel, I determined to find
my staff. Suddenly, I felt a yank on my suit coat
pocket. It was the man in the interview shoving
something into my coat. He left rather hurriedly,
and I reached into my coat pocket. It was a check
for $1,000.

The same voice of the Holy Spirit spoke, "How
would you like to be at the *right place*...at the right
time...every day of your life?" Again, I assured Him
that I would love to be at the right place...every
hour of my life!

If no one else ever tells you, the most powerful
and The Master Key to *One Thousand Times More*
is total and absolute *obedience* to the Voice of the
Holy Spirit...hourly.

58 Important Facts About
The Master Key Of Obedience

1.   *Obedience Is Doing Anything God*

Commands You To Do, Regardless Of The Cost Or Consequences. Jesus taught it. "If ye love Me, keep My commandments" (John 14:15).

2. *Obedience To The Word Of God Is The Only Duty Of Man.* "Let us hear the conclusion of the whole matter: Fear God, and keep His commandments: for this is the whole duty of man. For God shall bring every work into judgment, with every secret thing, whether it be good, or whether it be evil" (Ecclesiastes 12:13,14). This Scripture has been so important to me. It was the first Scripture I placed on the wall of my Secret Place, my private place of prayer.

3. *Your Obedience Is The Only Evidence That You Truly Know God.* John taught this key. "And hereby we do know that we know Him, if we keep His commandments" (1 John 2:3).

4. *Obedience Is An Hourly Event On The Path To One Thousand Times More.* The Apostle Paul wrote, "For as many as are led by the Spirit of God, they are the sons of God" (Romans 8:14).

"The Lord your God hath multiplied you, and, behold, ye are this day as the stars of heaven for multitude. (The Lord God of your fathers make you a thousand times so many more as ye are, and bless you, as He hath promised you!)" (Deuteronomy 1:10,11). Your agenda for today should be decided in the presence of God. Your daily schedule will create miracles or mistakes, tragedies or triumphs depending on whether or not you are led by the Spirit of God. *Hourly.* Your inner *peace* is a signal. Do not make a telephone call, an appointment or a decision unless you have peace in your heart about it.

5. *The Instructions Of God Are Never Unreasonable.* The Apostle Paul spoke, "I beseech you therefore, brethren, by the mercies of God, that ye present your bodies a living sacrifice, holy, acceptable unto God, which is your *reasonable* service" (Romans 12:1).

6. *Your Mind Requires Daily Renewing For Daily Obedience To The Continual Instructions Of God.* Paul taught this. "And be not conformed to this world: but be ye transformed by the renewing of your mind, that ye may prove what is that good, and acceptable, and perfect, will of God" (Romans 12:2). That is why I focus each morning on hearing the Scriptures on cassette tape. His Word washes my mind, my thoughts and the meditation of my heart. *It is the greatest success habit on earth.* You cannot have a great life until you have a pure life. You cannot have a pure life unless you have a pure mind. You cannot have a pure mind until it is washed with the Word of God *daily.*

7. *Nothing Offered As A Substitution For Your Obedience Will Be Accepted By God.* The Prophet Samuel taught this. "And Samuel said, Hath the Lord as great delight in burnt offerings and sacrifices, as in obeying the voice of the Lord? Behold, to obey is better than sacrifice, and to hearken than the fat of rams" (1 Samuel 15:22).

8. *Your Obedience Is The Miracle Magnet That Keeps The Presence Of God Around You.* "Lord, who shall abide in Thy tabernacle? who shall dwell in Thy holy hill? He that walketh uprightly, and worketh righteousness, and

speaketh the truth in his heart" (Psalm 15:1,2).

9. *Your Obedience To The Laws Of God Will Require Your Personal Knowledge Of The Laws Of God.* That is why the Apostle Paul Mentored Timothy in pursuing the Wisdom of God. "Study to shew thyself approved unto God, a workman that needeth not to be ashamed, rightly dividing the word of truth" (2 Timothy 2:15).

10. *Your Obedience To His Instruction Is The Only Proof Of Your Love For God.* Jesus taught this. "He that hath My commandments, and keepeth them, he it is that loveth Me:" (John 14:21).

John embraced this principle. "But whoso keepeth His word, in him verily is the love of God perfected: hereby know we that we are in Him" (1 John 2:5).

11. *Disobedience To God Always Produces Devastating Consequences.* "Then shall they call upon Me, but I will not answer; they shall seek Me early, but they shall not find Me: For that they hated knowledge, and did not choose the fear of the Lord: Therefore shall they eat of the fruit of their own way, and be filled with their own devices" (Proverbs 1:28,29,31).

Isaiah warned: "But if ye refuse and rebel, ye shall be devoured with the sword: for the mouth of the Lord hath spoken it" (Isaiah 1:20).

12. *Your Obedience Guarantees That God Will Always Respond Favorably To Your Requests.* "And whatsoever we ask, we receive of Him, because we keep His commandments, and do those things that are pleasing in His sight" (1 John 3:22).

The favor of God is the greatest force necessary to produce the Harvest of *One Thousand*

Times More.

13. *Obedience Is The Proof You Are Truly A Child Of God.* Jesus spoke, "My sheep hear My voice, and I know them, and they follow Me:" (John 10:27).

14. *The Word Of God Is The Voice Of God You Must Obey.* Peter explained it clearly. "We have also a more sure word of prophecy; whereunto ye do well that ye take heed, as unto a light that shineth in a dark place, until the day dawn, and the day star arise in your hearts: Knowing this first, that no prophecy of the scripture is of any private interpretation. For the prophecy came not in old time by the will of man: but holy men of God spake as they were moved by the Holy Ghost" (2 Peter 1:19-21).

15. *The Greatest Quality Of Jesus Was His Obedience To The Will Of The Father.* Paul wrote, "But made Himself of no reputation, and took upon Him the form of a servant, and was made in the likeness of men: And being found in fashion as a man, He humbled Himself, and became obedient unto death, even the death of the cross" (Philippians 2:7,8).

16. *Promotion Always Follows Your Obedience.* It happened in the life of Jesus. As Paul wrote, "And being found in fashion as a man, He humbled Himself, and became obedient unto death, even the death of the cross. Wherefore God also hath highly exalted Him, and given Him a name which is above every name:" (Philippians 2:8,9).

17. *Jesus Considered His Acts Of Obedience To Be An Example For Your Obedience.* "Ye call Me

Master and Lord: and ye say well; for so I am. If I then, your Lord and Master, have washed your feet; ye also ought to wash one another's feet. For I have given you an example, that ye should do as I have done to you. Verily, verily, I say unto you, The servant is not greater than his lord; neither he that is sent greater than he that sent him" (John 13:13-16).

18. *When You Obey An Instruction From God, Joy Will Result And Be The Proof Of His Pleasure In You.* "If ye know these things, happy are ye if ye do them" (John 13:17). "...he that keepeth the law, happy is he" (Proverbs 29:18).

19. *Jesus Guaranteed That He Would Personally Live In The Heart Of Anyone Who Was Obedient.* "If a man love Me, he will keep My words: and My Father will love him, and We will come unto him, and make Our abode with him" (John 14:23).

20. *Your Obedience Guarantees The Friendship Of God.* "Ye are My friends, if ye do whatsoever I command you" (John 15:14).

21. *Obedience Is The Proof Of Love.* "Jesus answered and said unto him, If a man love Me, he will keep My words: and My Father will love him, and We will come unto him, and make Our abode with him. He that loveth me not keepeth not My sayings: and the word which ye hear is not Mine, but the Father's which sent Me" (John 14:23,24).

22. *Your Obedience To Any Instruction From God Will Create Remarkable And Indescribable Peace.* Jesus promised, "Peace I leave with you, My peace I give unto you: not as the world giveth, give I unto you" (John 14:27). The Apostle Paul wrote,

"And let the peace of God rule in your hearts," (Colossians 3:15).

Focusing on God and His word creates peace of mind. The Prophet Isaiah said, "Thou wilt keep him in perfect peace, whose mind is stayed on Thee: because he trusteth in Thee" (Isaiah 26:3).

23. *Obedience Does Not Always Appear Logical To The Natural Mind Of Man.* "There is a way which seemeth right unto a man, but the end thereof are the ways of death" (Proverbs 14:12). Sometimes what God tells you to do will appear illogical and even ridiculous. It may even deprive you of an immediate gratification. It may wound your pride. Sometimes, an instruction seems totally unrelated to the miracle you are pursuing, but it will *always* be rewarded.

When Joshua wanted to defeat Jericho, an illogical instruction came. Walk around the walls of Jericho seven days in a row, and then, seven times on Sunday. Jesus instructed a blind man to wash clay and spittle from his eyes in the pool of Siloam. It was two miles away and seemingly an absurd request. But, the *obedience* was proof that the blind man *believed* the instructions of Jesus. Miracles come to the obedient, not the logical.

24. *It Is Not Impossible To Obey God.* "For this is the love of God, that we keep His commandments: and His commandments are not grievous" (1 John 5:3). Jesus declared clearly, "For My yoke is easy, and My burden is light" (Matthew 11:30).

25. *God Will Never Advance You Beyond Your Last Act Of Disobedience.* Joshua discovered this. After their horrifying losses in the battle of Ai, he cried out to God. But, one of his people had defied

an instruction from God. Joshua discovered some-thing few understand: *Individual Disobedience Can Create Corporate Punishment.* Every promo-tion was paralyzed. God spoke to Joshua, "Get thee up; wherefore liest thou thus upon thy face? Israel hath sinned, and they have also transgressed My covenant which I commanded them: for they have even taken of the accursed thing, and have also stolen, and dissembled also, and they have put it even among their own stuff" (Joshua 7:10,11). When Joshua made it right with God, penalized the rebel, God resumed the victories and promotion for Joshua and the Israelites.

26. *God Has Personally Guaranteed The Defeat Of Anyone Who Persists In Disobedience.* Your disobedience disappoints the heart of God. It stops the blessing. "Moreover all these curses shall come upon thee, and shall pursue thee, and over-take thee, till thou be destroyed; because thou hearkenedst not unto the voice of the Lord thy God, to keep His commandments and His statutes which He commanded thee:" (Deuteronomy 28:45).

God is always against sin because *sin has always destroyed what He loves the most,* you and me. Sin is heartache to God. Confront it. Uproot it. Ask His forgiveness. Do it now, even while you are reading these words.

27. *Your Obedience Is Rewarded With Super-natural Protection.* God promised this to Israel. "But if thou shalt indeed obey His voice, and do all that I speak; then I will be an enemy unto thine enemies, and an adversary unto thine adversaries" (Exodus 23:22). Satan will make every attempt to destroy you. Job illustrates this in the great

scenario of sorrow and restoration in his life. You are not capable of protecting yourself. Those who love you are incapable of protecting you from every adversary and satanic assault. But, God has *guaranteed your protection* as a reward for your personal obedience to His laws and principles.

28. *Your Obedience Is The Proof You Trust The Promises Of God To You.* God longs to be believed. "But without faith it is impossible to please Him; for he that cometh to God must believe that He is, and that He is a rewarder of them that diligently seek Him" (Hebrews 11:6).

29. *Uncommon Obedience Always Creates Uncommon Miracles.* Abraham is a marvelous example. Sarah was too old to produce a child. But Abraham believed God. "Through faith also Sarah herself received strength to conceive seed, and was delivered of a child when she was past age, because she judged Him faithful who had promised" (Hebrews 11:11; see also Romans 4:18-21).

30. *The Disobedience Of One Person Can Cause Tragedies For Thousands.* It happened when Achan sinned and kept the accursed thing, under the leadership of Joshua (see Joshua chapter 7). When Korah rebelled against the leadership of Moses, hundreds were destroyed because of it (see Numbers chapter 16). Adam introduced sorrow into the human race. Paul writes, "For as by one man's disobedience many were made sinners," (Romans 5:19).

31. *The Obedience Of One Person Can Bring Awesome Miracles To Thousands.* When Moses embraced the leadership of Israel in total obedience to God, millions were delivered. When David

accepted the challenge of Goliath, the Israelites went free. When Peter preached obediently on the day of Pentecost, thousands received and believed the message of Jesus. When the Apostle Paul surrendered obediently to the call of God, he rewrote the history of the church.

32. *Your Obedience To Tithe Faithfully Opens The Windows Of Heaven And Guarantees Supernatural Provision For Your Family.* Malachi declares, "Bring ye all the tithes into the storehouse, that there may be meat in Mine house, and prove Me now herewith, saith the Lord of hosts, if I will not open you the windows of heaven, and pour you out a blessing, that there shall not be room enough to receive it. And I will rebuke the devourer for your sakes, and he shall not destroy the fruits of your ground; neither shall your vine cast her fruit before the time in the field, saith the Lord of hosts" (Malachi 3:10,11).

33. *Your Obedience To Confront Strife Will Create Peace.* "Cast out the scorner, and contention shall go out; yea, strife and reproach shall cease" (Proverbs 22:10). Always mark contentious people. Do not give them an opportunity to poison your world. Take charge. Confront it. An answer comes and solutions *will emerge.*

34. *Your Obedience To Hear The Word Of God In Your Life Will Birth Great Faith Within You.* "So then faith cometh by hearing, and hearing by the word of God" (Romans 10:17). Someone said, "Faith comes when you hear God talk." What you read will affect what you believe. Feeding the Scriptures into your heart causes faith to come alive. *Faith is confidence in God.* When you hear

anything God is saying, faith will come alive in your heart. What You Keep Hearing, You Eventually Believe.

35. *Your Obedience To Forgive Others Guarantees God Will Forgive You.* "For if ye forgive men their trespasses, your heavenly Father will also forgive you: But if ye forgive not men their trespasses, neither will your Father forgive your trespasses" (Matthew 6:14,15).

36. *Your Obedience To Give Alms To The Unfortunate Guarantees Public Blessing From The Father.* "That thine alms may be in secret: and thy Father which seeth in secret Himself shall reward thee openly" (Matthew 6:4).

37. *Your Obedience To Sow Mercy And Forgiveness To Others Guarantees Mercy And Forgiveness Will Return To You From Others.* "Give, and it shall be given unto you; good measure, pressed down, and shaken together, and running over, shall men give into your bosom. For with the same measure that ye mete withal it shall be measured to you again" (Luke 6:38).

38. *Disobedience Will Always Bring The Chastening Of The Lord.* "For whom the Lord loveth He chasteneth, and scourgeth every son whom He receiveth. Now no chastening for the present seemeth to be joyous, but grievous: nevertheless afterward it yieldeth the peaceable fruit of righteousness unto them which are exercised thereby" (Hebrews 12:6,11). Endure correction. Wisdom begins with correction. Errors must be exposed. Mistakes must be faced. The person who corrected you the most is possibly the person you love the most. Hell is filled of people who rejected

correction. Heaven is filled of people who accepted it.

39. *Your Obedience To Pursue Wise Counsel Will Always Be Rewarded With Safety*. "Where no counsel is, the people fall: but in the multitude of counsellors there is safety" (Proverbs 11:14). Ignorance is deadly. Do not risk it. Listen to Godly Mentors. Somebody knows something that will help you survive and even succeed during the most painful seasons of your life.

40. *Your Obedience To Parental Authority Guarantees Uncommon Blessing For A Lifetime.* "Children, obey your parents in the Lord: for this is right. Honour thy father and mother; which is the first commandment with promise; That it may be well with thee, and thou mayest live long on the earth" (Ephesians 6:1-3).

41. *Your Obedience To Your Employer Guarantees Reward From God.* "Servants, be obedient to them that are your masters according to the flesh, with fear and trembling, in singleness of your heart, as unto Christ; Knowing that whatsoever good thing any man doeth, the same shall he receive of the Lord, whether he be bond or free" (Ephesians 6:5,8).

42. *Your Obedience To Treat Your Employees Fairly Assures Compensation From Your Spiritual Overseer, God.* "And, ye masters, do the same things unto them, forbearing threatening: knowing that your Master also is in heaven; neither is there respect of persons with Him" (Ephesians 6:9).

43. *Your Obedience To Make Good Things Happen To Others Will Bring A Blessing From God.* "Withhold not good from them to whom it is due,

when it is in the power of thine hand to do it" (Proverbs 3:27). The greatest success principle I have ever discovered in my life is—What You Make Happen For Others, God Will Make Happen For You (see Ephesians 6:8).

44. *Your Obedience To Put On The Whole Armor Of God Guarantees Your Ability To Withstand Through Any Crisis.* "Wherefore take unto you the whole armour of God, that ye may be able to withstand in the evil day, and having done all, to stand" (Ephesians 6:13).

45. *Your Obedience To Keep Your Personal Prayer Appointment With The Holy Spirit, Guarantees Uncommon And Total Joy.* "...in Thy presence is fulness of joy; at Thy right hand there are pleasures for evermore" (Psalm 16:11). David describes the rewards of His presence. "One thing have I desired of the Lord, that will I seek after; that I may dwell in the house of the Lord all the days of my life, to behold the beauty of the Lord, and to inquire in His temple" (Psalm 27:4).

46. *Your Obedience To Fear The Lord Births The Secrets Of God Within Your Life.* "What man is he that feareth the Lord? him shall He teach in the way that he shall choose. His soul shall dwell at ease; and his Seed shall inherit the earth. The secret of the Lord is with them that fear Him; and He will shew them His covenant" (Psalm 25:12-14).

47. *Your Obedience To Wait Patiently On The Timing Of God Guarantees The Goodness Of God.* "The Lord is good unto them that wait for Him, to the soul that seeketh Him. It is good that a man should both hope and quietly wait for the salvation of the Lord" (Lamentations 3:25,26).

48. *Your Obedience To Prophetic Authority Will Bring Uncommon Revelation And Blessing.* "Surely the Lord God will do nothing, but He revealeth His secret unto His servants the prophets" (Amos 3:7).

"Believe in the Lord your God, so shall ye be established; believe His prophets, so shall ye prosper" (2 Chronicles 20:20). When thousands sneer and laugh and jeer at a man of God speaking prophetically, others walk in that light and explode into uncommon promotion. It is One of the Master Keys to increasing your life—*One Thousand Times More.*

49. *Your Obedience To Sing, Praise And Worship God Positions God As An Adversary To Deal With Your Enemies And Bring Their Defeat.* "And when he had consulted with the people, he appointed singers unto the Lord, and that should praise the beauty of holiness, as they went out before the army, and to say, Praise the Lord; for His mercy endureth for ever. And when they began to sing and to praise, the Lord set ambushments against the children of Ammon, Moab, and mount Seir, which were come against Judah; and they were smitten" (2 Chronicles 20:21,22).

50. *Your Obedience To Pastoral Authority Brings Blessing.* "Obey them that have the rule over you, and submit yourselves: for they watch for your souls, as they that must give account, that they may do it with joy, and not with grief: for that is unprofitable for you" (Hebrews 13:17).

51. *Your Obedience To Sever Wrong Relationships Prevents Tragedy.* You see, every act

of obedience produces an inevitable reward. "And have no fellowship with the unfruitful works of darkness, but rather reprove them" (Ephesians 5:11). Samson was disobedient and lost the status of championship. His eyes were gouged out, and he became the laughing stock of the Philistines. Disobedience is costly. Embarrassing. Humiliating. Unnecessary. "Be not deceived: evil communications corrupt good manners" (1 Corinthians 15:33).

52. *Your Obedience To Rely Totally On The Word Of God Creates Uncommon Favor.* "...but let thine heart keep My commandments; For length of days, and long life, and peace, shall they add to thee. Let not mercy and truth forsake thee: bind them about thy neck; write them upon the table of thine heart: So shalt thou find favour and good understanding in the sight of God and man" (Proverbs 3:1-4).

53. *Your Obedience To Honor God With The Firstfruits Of Any Financial Blessing Guarantees Uncommon Financial Prosperity.* "Honour the Lord with thy substance, and with the firstfruits of all thine increase: So shall thy barns be filled with plenty, and thy presses shall burst out with new wine" (Proverbs 3:9,10).

54. *Obedience To Stay Humble Toward God And Fear Him In Avoiding Evil Even Affects Your Health.* "Be not wise in thine own eyes: fear the Lord, and depart from evil. It shall be health to thy navel, and marrow to thy bones" (Proverbs 3:7,8).

55. *Your Obedience To Pursue Wisdom As The Principle Focus Of Your Life Guarantees*

Continuous Joy And Victory. "Happy is the man that findeth wisdom, and the man that getteth understanding. Her ways are ways of pleasantness, and all her paths are peace. She is a tree of life to them that lay hold upon her: and happy is every one that retaineth her" (Proverbs 3:13, 17,18).

56. *God Often Permits Adversity To Unlock A Desire To Obey And To Learn His Laws.* "It is good for me that I have been afflicted; that I might learn Thy statutes" (Psalm 119:71).

57. *When You Are At The Place Of Obedience, The Right People Move Toward You.* When Ruth obediently adapted to the schedule of Naomi, Boaz emerged. When Elijah went to Zarephath, the widow emerged. When Esther obeyed the instructions of Mordecai, the king showed favor.

58. *Provision is Only Guaranteed At Your Place Of Obedience.* Ruth had to be at the place where Boaz could see her. Joseph had to be seen by Pharaoh before he was promoted. Esther had to be seen by the king. It is important to always be at the very place, the job, the company or even the town God wants you. If you are not where God has assigned you, start moving in that direction. Secure counsel from your Mentors, your boss, your family.

Develop a passion for hourly obedience to the Inner Voice of your greatest Advisor and Mentor, the Holy Spirit.

It is the Master Key to the promise of *One Thousand Times More.*

✎ 6 ✎

CREATE YOUR DAILY SUCCESS ROUTINE.

Great Men Have Great Habits.

In California, a powerful spiritual leader awakens at 5:30 a.m. each day. He has followed this routine for years. He prays from 5:30 to 6:30 a.m. *every morning* of his life. It is a *daily* habit—the success habit that has unlocked an unforgettable anointing for teaching. He walks, lives and breathes the atmosphere of *One Thousand Times More.* Is it a mystery? Not really. When your Daily Success Routine begins with the first hour of every day in the presence of God, it is almost impossible to fail.

One of the most famous business women on earth lived here in Dallas, Texas. She was worth over 300 million dollars and her business is worth over 2 billion. She had a daily Success Routine. Since 1962, she would write her daily plan on a sheet of paper.

She listed only six tasks for the day.

She worked on the first, then the second, then the third, and so forth. She believed that one of The Master Keys to her uncommon success was this constant and consistent daily habit. *Planning was her daily routine.*

A former Presidential Chief-of-Staff revealed part of his Daily Success Routine. The *first* thing he did every morning and the *last* thing he did every night was to plan the day of the President. It was his habit.

One of the wealthiest athletes in history revealed a few weeks ago that the morning after he won the heavyweight championship of the world, he was back in his gym...his Daily Success Routine. The morning after! Millions of dollars were earned within minutes. But, he knew and had decided for his life, the *daily habits* necessary to create the *future* he loved.

One famous Hall Of Fame baseball pitcher pitched his seventh no-hitter. Afterwards, reporters found him in the locker room doing what he always did—riding a stationary bike for one hour and fifteen minutes. He had just pitched a no-hitter! Did he race out and do something exciting and different? He did not become a champion by chasing after every thought fleeting through his mind. He became a champion through his Daily Success Routine. He had developed the *Habits for Greatness.*

Habit is the most misunderstood word in the English language. When someone talks about habits, everyone thinks about drugs, alcohol or smoking. They think habit is a word connected to something evil, deteriorating or deadly.

Habit is a good word, a powerful gift from God. Habit simply means that when you do something twice, it becomes easier. It is a gift from God enabling us to succeed.

Personal hygiene habits increase your health, self-confidence and social influence.

Conversation habits strengthen relationships, build confidence and integrity.

Financial habits can create uncommon increase, yes, *One Thousand Times More.*

Discipline is different than habit. God did not create us to be creatures of discipline but creatures of *habit.*

The purpose of discipline is to birth a habit.

Psychologists say that when you perform an act for 21 consecutive days without fail, it will become a habit.

Habits create a future you will love or hate.

Habit is the child of purpose, destiny and desire. Let me give you an example. When Mohammed Ali, the great boxer, believed that destiny and God had determined his future would be the greatest boxer on earth, his habits *changed.* He arose earlier. His workouts were more intense. His conversation changed. Yes, he even changed his name! You see, your habits are the results of your beliefs of what you truly believe you deserve to possess and have.

Desires birth habits. Some who have smoked for 40 years quit in a week when the doctor revealed that they were standing at the door of death.

Thirty years ago, I sat at the table of a pastor friend in Louisiana. I stared at him and asked, "How on earth did you become so huge?" (He weighed 400 pounds!)

"Eating every night after church just like you are eating right now," he said boldly.

I laughed. I thought he was simply a little peeved at my bluntness. But, he was sincere. (Unfortunately, I stayed ignorant!) What he really said to me was, "I have an eating routine. Every night, after I have spent a long day in work and effort, I sit at this table and comfort myself with food. *It is a habit in my life.* I didn't *begin* this big. It didn't happen within a few days. My habit of eating after church at night added a pound, another pound, and another pound."

Your habits have created your present physical condition. Whether you are overweight, unhealthy or uncommonly strong, what you keep eating *daily* is creating the You-In-The-Future. What you eat is increasing your health or decreasing your health.

Your spending habits are creating a secure financial future or destroying it completely. A friend of mine told me that a simple saving of $100 invested in mutual funds, *every month*...would result in a baby becoming a millionaire at 20 years old. Just $100...monthly. Habits create paupers or millionaires.

Here Are 14 Wisdom Keys On Developing Your Daily Success Routine

1. Men Do Not Decide Their Future, They Decide The Habits That Determine Their Future.

2. What You Do *Daily* Is Deciding What You Are Becoming *Permanently.*

3.   Nothing Will Ever Dominate Your Life Unless It Happens *Daily.*

4.   You Cannot Change Your Life Until You Change Something You Keep Doing...*Daily.*

5.   You Can Trace The Failure Of Every Man To Something He Permitted To Occur *Daily* In His Life, *Body Or His Mind.*

6.   You Can Trace Uncommon Success To Habits That Were Created...A Daily Success Routine.

7.   Your Habits Are Creating Increase Or Decrease.

8.   Your Habits Are Being Strengthened Or Changed By The Friends You Permit Daily Close To You.

9.   What You Keep Looking At Is Deciding Where You Will Go.

10. Gaze Only Upon That Which You Desire In Your Future.

11. You Will Always Move Toward The Dominant Picture In Your Mind. That is why it is important that you place pictures around you of the things you desire to move toward and have.

12. You Can Change A Failure Routine Into A Success Routine Within 21 Days.

13. What You Keep Doing Daily Is Creating The Future You Have Always Wanted Or The Future You Dread.

14. Your Money Habits Are Making You A Pauper Or A Millionaire.

In the Ancient Writings, there are several photographs of people who had success habits and routines. Jesus went *regularly* to the synagogue.

David prayed *seven times* each day. Daniel prayed *three times* each day. Zacharias offered up sacrifices, as *was his custom*.

Your Daily Success Routine is affecting the Promise of *One Thousand Times More*.

Here Are 7 Daily Habits I Have Recognized In The Lives Of Uncommon Men And Women

1.   *Uncommon Achievers Arise At The Same Time Every Morning*.   John R. Rice, the famous Baptist evangelist of many years ago, would often arrive home from his crusades at 3:00 or 4:00 a.m., on Monday mornings. But his staff declared, "Regardless of when he arrived, he was at the office the same time each morning!"

2.   *Uncommon Men Start Their Work At The Same Time Each Day*.   One of my close friends told me, "The wealthiest man in our town backs out of his driveway at 7:55 a.m. every morning...without fail. Mike, I can set my clock by it." He has a Daily Success Routine.

Ernest Hemingway, the famed writer, wrote every night from midnight until 6:00 a.m. in the morning, then he would sleep from 6:00 a.m. to 2:00 p.m. in the afternoon. The most prolific writers in America have a Daily Success Routine, writing the same hours every day.

3.   *Uncommon Men Pray At The Same Time Every Day*.   David did. "Early will I seek Thee." Daniel prayed three times a day. Always establish a consistent appointment in The Secret Place.   It

will radically change your life. It may be for five minutes, but do it daily. It must become a part of your Daily Success Routine.

4. *Uncommon Men Read The Word Of God Daily As A Part Of Their Success Routine.* Reading three chapters a day (and five on Sundays) enables you to complete the Bible once a year. If you keep waiting until you have time, you will never read it. Your success routine in the Word will keep storing within you the thoughts and presence of God. *Nothing is more important than your appointment in The Secret Place each day reading the Word of God.*

My greatest success habit is *listening to the Bible every morning* on tape or CD when I awaken. It is the first thing I do every day even before I brush my teeth. His Word washes my mind, stimulates my faith, and puts a picture of my Best Friend before me, the Holy Spirit.

5. *Uncommon Champions Habitually Speak Words Of Hope, Confidence And Expectation Of Excellence.* Words create your future.

Your words of faith and enthusiasm are the fuel unleashing the promised Harvest of *One Thousand Times More.*

6. *Uncommon Achievers Have A Habit Of Planning Their Day.* The late Mary Kay Ash, the famed multimillionaire, planned every day with a simple list of six things to do. Mark McCormack invests *one hour* every morning in planning the next 23 hours. Think about it! He plans his day for one solid hour before doing anything else.

7. *Uncommon Leaders Exercise Every Day*

Of Their Life. President Harry Truman walked an hour every day until he was almost 80 years old. He had determined the Daily Success Routine of his future.

> ▶ How passionate are you about the *One Thousand Times More* Health? You must create the Daily Success Routine that moves you toward that Harvest.

> ▶ How passionate are you about *One Thousand Times More* Wisdom? You must include Mentorship every single day...as part of your Daily Success Routine.

> ▶ How passionate are you about *One Thousand Times More* Finances? You must invest time in creating a Daily Success Routine every day of your life...in financial Mentorship, focus on an Uncommon Dream and strengthen the relationships that create increase...every day.

How passionate are you in unleashing *One Thousand Times More* Favor than you have ever known? You must *sow* favor every single day...as a part of your Daily Success Routine.

When I began to meditate, read and study the Laws of Increase, many keys appeared: Tenacity, Integrity, Motivation and scores of others. When I determined to recognize the seven most powerful keys, it exploded...The Daily Success Routine.

It has been ignored in most motivation books.

Now, what really causes a man to reverse the bad habits of his life and birth new ones? A tragedy in his life? A screaming mate? Not really. You simply have an awakening of a dormant, ignored, overlooked *Dream within you of how great your life can really become. You need a Dream.*

An Uncommon Dream.

▶ You cannot change your life until you change your *habits*.

▶ You cannot change your habits until you change your *Dream*.

▶ You will not change your Dream until you become angry with your present.

Are you feeling pain? You are ready for the Promise of *One Thousand Times More.*

I read an interesting statistic a few weeks ago in a powerful book on millionaires in America. It showed how the wealthiest people in America, by percentages, were people from *other countries* who entered the United States *impoverished*. Their past was so painful and so powerful in their mind, they developed work and money habits that created incredible success. The book also explained how the middle-class American has almost no chance at wealth, *because he is not feeling enough pain.*

4 Important Facts You Should Know About Pain

▶ Your pain determines your *motivation*.

▶ Your pain determines your *focus*.

▶ Your pain determines *who* you pursue.

▶ Your pain determines the Wisdom you believe is *worthy of pursuit*.

It will take more than a miracle anointing service, a self-help improvement book or a network marketing plan to unleash *One Thousand Times More* finances.

It will take more than an exercise guru on television, a new jogging suit or a free membership at the gym...to unlock *One Thousand Times More* health.

It will take more than six tapes from a marriage counselor, a bouquet of roses or a pretty negligée...to unlock *One Thousand Times More* passion in your marriage.

It will require total focus on creating your Daily Success Routine.

What You Keep Doing Daily Is Creating The Future You Have Always Wanted Or The Future You Dread.

When you change your daily routine, you can unlock the Promise of *One Thousand Times More* for your family, your pastor and the work of God.

Your Dream Is Deciding Your Habits.

How To Create Your Daily Success Routine

1.   *Recognize What Is Worthy Of Your Total Focus Today.* Everyone will have a different focus. You must target what you desire the most. Permit others to stay in the center of their focus.

2.   *Pinpoint The Top Three Distractions That Occur Habitually.* The Only Reason Men Fail Is Broken Focus. Satan cannot destroy you, merely *distract* you. You can trace any failure to loss of focus. What breaks your focus daily on the things you love the most? Who can help you *protect* your focus?

3. *Pray Continuously In The Holy Spirit.* He has an agenda. You must discern His, not decide your own.

4. *Determine The Core Product Of Your Life.* What do you want to do the most? What is the *legacy* you desire to leave? What are you willing to walk away from to see it take place?

Everything does not have equal value.

Everyone does not deserve equal time.

5. *Embrace Flexibility As An Opportunity.* Hillary Rodham Clinton once said, "I've never had a plan yet where everything happened as I planned it." You can take advantage of the unexpected.

6. *Recognize Those Around You Who Do Not Have A Determined Focus Or Goal.* They want your attention and do not hesitate to break your focus.

7. *Discern Those Who Are Oblivious And Blind Toward Your Focus.* I have been dictating books and have "friends" burst into the room distracting me with trivia. Confront rudeness.

8. *Keep A Visual Picture Of Your Desired Goal And Dream Before You.* Gyms have pictures of physical champions who have won Mr. USA, Miss America, and so forth, in front of them as motivation.

Abraham had a picture of the stars and the sand of the sea as personal motivation for his generations of children. Joseph had a picture of himself in authority. Jesus had a picture of returning to the Father.

9. *Become Militant About Keeping Your Daily Success Routine.* One of the happiest sea-

sons of my life was 12 years ago. I birthed a Daily Success Routine. I went to bed at 10:30 p.m. with a cup of hot chocolate. I arose at 5:30 and walked three miles in the morning and three miles at night. My joy was remarkable. My peace was unexplainable. After several weeks, a friend rushed into my hotel room. He wanted me to help him work on a special letter to his congregation and partners. I told him about my Daily Success Routine. It was late. I needed to sleep. He laughed it off and kept talking.

He finally left at 1:00 a.m.

My entire rhythm was affected. Quite deeply. I was unable to arise at 5:30 the next morning and pray, so I decided I would pray at 8:00 a.m. Every appointment the next day had to be changed. Something was lost that I cannot explain. It never came back for many, many months.

A good habit is too powerful to treat lightly. Become militant about keeping it.

What You Look At The Longest Will Become The Strongest.

Here Are 4 Powerful Rewards Of Focus

1. *Focus Keeps You Passionate About Your Goals.* Unclutter your life of anything or anyone that does not respect your focus. They dilute your passion, the only fuel available for the Uncommon Dreams of your heart.

2. *Focus Will Keep You Creative.* What you keep studying, observing and examining—you will become creative toward. Have you ever looked at your house and kept thinking of different ways to

arrange the furniture? The longer you looked, the more ideas emerged. One of my best friends is Gloria Kelso, an incredible Interior Decorator from Nashville, Tennessee. Recently, she told me she wanted to help advise me on redecorating my home—free of charge as a Seed into my life. As she spent day after day, focusing completely on re-designing my house, her ideas astounded me. She literally created "another world" for me. *Focus unleashed her creativity.*

3. *Focus Keeps You Persistent.* When you are focused on a goal, tenacity multiplies. Persistence is birthed.

4. *Focus Alienates The Unnecessary From Your Life.* You must constantly remind yourself.

Some things matter for an *hour.*

Some things matter for *today.*

Some things matter *forever.*

Some things do not really matter at *all.*

10 Incredible Ways Words Can Affect The Promise Of One Thousand Times More

1. *Right Words Can Turn An Angry Man Into A Friend.* "A soft answer turneth away wrath:" (Proverbs 15:1).

2. *Right Words Will Breathe Energy And Life Into Everything Around You.* "A wholesome tongue is a tree of life:" (Proverbs 15:4).

3. *Right Words Can Energize And Motivate Your Own Life.* "A man hath joy by the answer of his mouth: and a word spoken in due season, how good is it!" (Proverbs 15:23).

4.   *Right Words Decide Which Dreams Live And Which Dreams Die.* "Death and life are in the power of the tongue: and they that love it shall eat the fruit thereof" (Proverbs 18:21).

5.   *Right Words Are As Important As Silver And Gold.* "The tongue of the just is as choice silver:" (Proverbs 10:20).

6.   *Right Words Can Get You Out Of Trouble.* "...but the mouth of the upright shall deliver them" (Proverbs 12:6).

7.   *Right Words Can Bring Health And Healing.* "...the tongue of the wise is health" (Proverbs 12:18).

8.   *Right Words Can Open Doors To Powerful, Important And Influential Leaders.* "Righteous lips are the delight of kings; and they love him that speaketh right" (Proverbs 16:13).

9.   *Right Words Can Cure Bitterness.* "Pleasant words are as an honeycomb, sweet to the soul, and health to the bones" (Proverbs 16:24).

10.   *Right Words Can Unlock A Financial Raise Or Promotion.* "A man's belly shall be satisfied with the fruit of his mouth; and with the increase of his lips shall he be filled" (Proverbs 18:20). *Uncommon achievers place great importance on your ability to speak right words.* Dave Thomas, the beloved founder of Wendy's International, said in his book, *"Well Done"* (page 136), "Communication is the heart of success."

Your daily words affect your success.

Create the Daily Success Routine and you can unleash the Promise of *One Thousand Times More.*

☜ 7 ☞

Sow Uncommon Seeds Expectantly.

You Will Reap What You Sow.

Scriptures prove it. "Be not deceived; God is not mocked: for whatsoever a man soweth, that shall he also reap" (Galatians 6:7).

Here Are 71 Facts You Should Know About Sowing Your Way To One Thousand Times More...The Journey Of The Seed!

1. *Every Person On Earth Understands The Law Of Sowing And Reaping.* The farmer stands as a monument to the powerful law of reproduction. When you sow a kernel of corn, you will produce corn. When you sow a tomato seed, you will produce a tomato. When a man plants his seed into his wife, he will produce a child.

2. *Seed-Faith Is The Principle That You Can Produce Anything You Want In Your Future From Something You Are Holding Today.* That is the principle! You can decide the Harvest you desire and plant a specific Seed toward that Harvest.

3. *Someone Close To You Who Is In Trouble*

Is Potential Soil For Your Seed. Your Seed of love, time, encouragement, prayers and finances. Jesus explained that when you have done something good to others, you were making it happen for Him.

4. *Your Seed Is Anything That Blesses Somebody.* It is anything that improves the life of someone you love or know. Your *Seed* is whatever you do that makes another smile, laugh, feel good or satisfied. Your Seed is anything that is making someone's life much easier.

Your Seed is anything you *know,* possess or can do for another that increases their joy.

Thoughts are Seeds.

Love is a Seed.

Time is a Seed.

Patience is a Seed.

Mercy is a Seed.

Kindness is a Seed.

Money is a Seed.

Your prayers are Seeds.

Thankfulness is a Seed.

Your *Seed* is anything you have received from God that He wants you to impart into someone else.

5. *The Law Of Sowing And Reaping Was Intended To Birth Encouragement, Hope And Excitement About A Harvest.* "And let us not be weary in well doing: for in due season we shall reap, if we faint not" (Galatians 6:9).

6. *Your Seed Is Any Tool God Has Given You To Create Your Future.* Look at David. He complained about the armor of Saul. But, he had another tool—the slingshot. It was simple.

Overlooked. Ignored by other soldiers. But, it was the *Seed* that God had placed in his hand. It was his supernatural tool! God always leaves you with *something*. What is it? *Find it.*

7. *God Always Gives You Something To Begin Your Future.* David had a *slingshot* to create a victory. The widow had a *meal* to invest into a man of God. You have *something!* Look for it again!

8. *There Will Never Be A Day In Your Life That You Have Nothing.* You may be impoverished like the widow. Many think she had nothing. She had something—powerful, incredible and rare. She had the ability to *discern* a man of God. She had the ability to *listen* to a man of God. She had the ability to *obey* a man of God.

9. *A Little Seed Can Birth A Huge Harvest.* Acorns become oak trees. Babies become champions. You are a living collection of *Seeds.* You contain a million tiny, golden, passionate *Beginnings* for change.

10. *Something You Have Been Given By God Will Create Anything Else You Have Ever Been Promised By God.* Tenacity in the woman who hemorrhaged for a dozen years, created the miracle of touching the hem of Jesus' garment. The loaves and fishes of a small lad created enough for the multitude. Stop looking at what others possess. Instead, start thanking God for something He has already given you.

11. *Every Seed Contains A Billion, Tiny, Golden, Passionate Beginnings Of Miracles.* Someone counted 470 seeds in a single papaya. My

longtime friend, Dwight Thompson told me that one papaya seed produces a plant that contains ten papayas. Imagine the seeds if every papaya in one plant contained 470! Ten papaya seeds containing 470 seeds is 4,700 papaya seeds! Now, imagine replanting those 4,700 papaya seeds to create 4,700 papaya plants.

Let's round it off. Five thousand papaya plants containing 5,000 seeds on each plant is 25 million papaya seeds! Incredible! Think about it for a moment. One papaya seed can produce a plant with almost 5,000 seeds. Those 5,000 seeds produce another 5,000 plants that contain together (if all the numbers were accurate) 25 million more seeds! Each of those seeds contains millions of passionate *Beginnings* for change.

12. *You Are A Walking Warehouse Of Remarkable Seeds.* Most people have no idea what they contain! They waste thousands of hours studying their losses instead of taking inventory of what they have been given. They look at what they have *not* instead of what they have *got*.

Listen carefully. It is rarely destructive or devastating to take an inventory of all the things you need and desire. But, it is tragic beyond words if you fail to *recognize your Seeds*—what you have received from God to plant into the lives of others. Stop focusing on losses. Look longer, closer and thankfully at something you have already been given and presently have.

Moses could not talk well. But, God turned his focus away from his need and invited him to acknowledge the rod in his hand.

His rod was his Seed.

13. *Those Around You Are The Soil Designed To Receive Your Seeds.* "As we have therefore opportunity, let us do good unto all men, especially unto them who are of the household of faith" (Gal. 6:10).

14. *Something You Already Possess Is Your Key To Your Future.* It may be knowledge, money, skills or ideas, insights and concepts. But, you already have enough to create your future. It will launch the *One Thousand Times More.*

15. *You Often May Need Someone To Ignite Your Faith To Unlock The Seeds You Already Possess.* The widow needed Elijah. Without others around you to motivate you, encourage you and unlock something in your faith—your Seeds will go unplanted. Your Harvest will never be experienced. That is why obedience is so necessary. It links you with the *right* people, who unleash your faith.

16. *Everything You Have Was Given To You By God.* Do not become cocky over tithing your small amount of ten percent. Your *entire* paycheck came from God! Your *eyesight* came from God! Your *hearing* came from God! Your *health* came from God! Your *intelligence* came from God! Your *favor* from others came from God! You do not have a thing that God did not give you.

17. *When You Let Go Of What Is In Your Hand, God Will Let Go Of What Is In His Hand.* When the small lad released the loaves and fishes into the hands of Jesus, Jesus released back into his loaves and fishes the multiplication began... miracle. And they picked up several baskets later!

18. *When You Keep What Is In Your Hand, God Will Keep What Is In His Hand.* If the widow had withheld from the man of God, she would have starved. The Windows of Blessing close when you close your bowels of compassion and you stop sowing Seeds of faith.

19. *If You Keep What You Presently Have, That Is The Most It Will Ever Be.* When you sow it, it is the least it will ever be. This is one of the most vital principles you must understand in unleashing *One Thousand Times More.* Releasing what you have is the only evidence of your faith that God will provide for you.

20. *Everything Within You Is A Seed Someone Has Sown Into You, With Or Without Your Permission.* Think back. Your parents sowed their love, attention and favor into you. Thousands of dollars have been poured into you from others when you were too small, too ignorant or too young to recognize it. Your teachers taught you the alphabet, numbers and how to *share.* Your education was a Seed into your life from every teacher.

21. *The Prophet Elijah Proved The Principle Of Seed-Faith To The Widow Of Zarephath.* She was impoverished and at the door of death. Her son was about to die. They had reached their last meal. But, the man of God showed up. He sowed the Seed of truth and faith regarding this principle—she was miraculously supplied with food for the rest of the famine because of her Seed. The prophet told her she would never lack if she sowed her Seed of Obedience. It happened.

22. *The Promise Of One Thousand Times*

More Can Only Occur When A Seed Of Obedience Has Been Planted. Seeds of faith, kindness, finances and love. Everything you have can produce a future. The *One Thousand Times More* is a Harvest. But, there will be a specific Seed that sets it in motion.

▶ You must learn to sow.

▶ You must learn to sow *Uncommon Seeds.*

▶ You must learn to sow with *great expectation.*

That is the mystery behind the *One Thousand Times More!*

23. *Your Seed Is Something Little That Can Become Huge Tomorrow.* The little slingshot of David was the golden scepter that brought him to kingship. Something ridiculous *today* is often revolutionary *tomorrow.*

24. *Your Seed Is The Only Proof You Have Mastered Greed.* Men hoard. Satan steals. God has the nature of giving. Giving is the only cure for greed. Your Seed is the proof that you have mastered hoarding, selfishness and greed.

25. *Some Seed In Your Present Will Soon Explode Into Something Magnificent In Your Future.* Picture the tiny lad sitting at the piano, practicing over and over his music. His family is agitated, his teacher is impatient, but one morning thousands open a newspaper to find he is the leading pianist of his country. His endorsement is sought. Millions buy his tapes. Why? Something small in his present became magnificent in his future.

26. *When You Increase The Size Of Your Seed,*

You Increase The Size Of Your Harvest. "But this I say, He which soweth sparingly shall reap also sparingly; and he which soweth bountifully shall reap also bountifully" (2 Corinthians 9:6).

27. *A Seed Of Nothing Guarantees A Season Of Nothing.* Years ago, the Holy Spirit spoke to me to plant a beautiful Mercedes into the life of another. I was angry at this person. I refused. I lost *A Thousand Times More.* I have wondered about that many times. If a Seed of *Something* can create *something,* it is quite obvious—a Seed of *Nothing* will create a Season of *Nothing* in your life.

28. *Your Seed Must Be Comparable To The Harvest You Are Desiring.* You cannot plant a Chevrolet and produce a Rolls Royce! You cannot plant a Seed of $1.00 and expect to be a millionaire 30 days later. Your Seed, the soil and time has everything to do with the size of your Harvest.

29. *Your Seed Will Shorten The Season Of Now.* Are you going through a trial? When you plant a Seed, you shorten the present season. You see, your Seed is a part of your present that you *transfer* and move into your future. Your Seed is birthing change.

30. *When You Get Involved With God's Dream, He Will Get Involved With Your Dream.* That is the power of sowing. You create a Covenant. Think of a tiny Seed that enters into a Covenant with the soil. Within weeks, they have cracked a concrete slab!! That is the power of Two...the Covenant. The widow invested in the work of God, Elijah. God, then, entered into a Covenant with her that she would never lack in the

famine (read 1 Kings 17).

31. *Nobody Else Can Sow Your Seed For You.* Your love, your finances, your mercy toward others. Nobody else can sow your Seeds! That is why *One Thousand Times More* is your personal choice! It explains how the poor can become prosperous; the rich can become admired. Nobody can stop your future from birthing—because nobody else is controlling the Seed you are sowing today! Your Harvest today is a photograph of your yesterday Seeds.

32. *Nobody Can Stop The Harvest Your Seed Has Commanded.* Satan tried to stop the best Seed God ever planted, Jesus. Read Matthew 4, the temptations on the Mount. Satan tried repeatedly to stop Jesus from completing the will of the Father. Jesus even wept in the garden later and asked the Father, if possible, to move the Cup of Suffering away from Him. But the Seed of God carried an irreversible, *unstoppable* Harvest—the redemption of mankind. Men did not plant the Seed. It was eternal Seed, holy Seed, righteous Seed.

33. *Every Seed Contains An Invisible Instruction.* You cannot see it. It is invisible to your natural eye. Yet, a small watermelon seed will follow that instruction and produce more watermelons. The tomato seed will create more tomatoes. Uncertainty does not exist. Each Seed contains a specific, precise and powerful Assignment. The Creator placed it inside. Many small Seeds have even broken through concrete sidewalks—the Assignment was stronger than any

Enemy placed around it.

34. *When You Give Your Seed A Specific Assignment, Incredible Faith Is Unleashed.* The widow was demoralized. But, the man of God gave her a Portrait of Possibility. She was encouraged to plant a Seed so she would not lack. She did. Faith was born. "And she went and did according to the saying of Elijah: and she, and he, and her house, did eat many days" (1 Kings 17:15).

35. *Your Seed Is Always The Door Out Of Trouble.* It was for the widow. It will be for you. It may be information, motivation or encouragement. But, if you will give it an Assignment, it will produce an exit from your present season of chaos.

36. *Giving Your Seed A Specific Assignment Will Greatly Affect Your Focus Of Your Faith.* Focus matters. The secret of the Law of Success is concentration. The Only Reason Men Fail Is Broken Focus. In 2 Samuel 24, David focused his Seed to stop the tragedy. (Over 70,000 people had died in 72 hours.) The Assignment was completed. The plague stopped. David had discovered the secret.

37. *Your Seed Is The Only Proof Of Expectation.* When the farmer sows his seed in the soil, expectation arises. That is why tithing and sowing are so powerful—they unleash expectation, the only magnet for *One Thousand Times More.*

Need does not attract God.

Anger does not attract God.

Expectation attracts God.

Remember, *Seed-Faith Is Sowing What You Have Been Given To Create Something Else You Have Been Promised.*

Seed-Faith Is Letting Go Of The Seen To Create The Unseen.

38. *You Are Never Closer To God Than When You Sow A Seed Inspired By A Man Of God.* Faith moments are miracle moments. When Elijah saw the face of the widow, she was one meal from death. This is not the kind of crisis that inspires giving. It inspires hoarding!

▶ When You Enter The Presence Of A Man Of God, You Will Begin To Hear, Feel And Know The Thoughts Of God.

▶ When You Enter The Presence Of A Man Of God, Anything Within You Unlike God Will Begin To React. It begins looking for an Exit or an Expression.

I was at a service one night when a woman suddenly spoke up. It was harsh, anger and full of vindictiveness. It was unfortunate and sad. Why couldn't she just sit there? You see, everything unlike God in her required an expression or an exit. She chose the path of expression. Eventually, we had to exit her from the service...against her will!

39. *Recognize The Seed You Have Already Received From God.* Your Seed is any gift, skill, talent that God has provided for you. He expects you to sow into the lives of others. Do not hide your Seed. Use it. "A man's gift maketh room for him, and bringeth him before great men" (Proverbs 18:16). Leaders always respond to your *difference* from others.

40. *Recognize With Thankfulness The Seeds Others Are Sowing Into Your Life Today.* The

widow of 1 Kings 17 was starving and impoverished. Her son was emaciated. They were at the
door of death. But, a man of God began to sow
Seeds of Wisdom, motivation and faith. Each
instruction was a Seed. Those instructions shifted
her focus to faith. Then, he painted an incredible
portrait on her mind—the Portrait of Possibility.
He showed her that she would not lack during the
entire famine...if she planted and sowed her Seed.
Elijah had no money. He had no house. But, he
sowed *Seeds of Truth* into a tormented mind, and
her defeated heart became victorious again. His
Seed was enough to create a Harvest.

41. *Sow Into Others What Nobody Else Is
Willing To Sow Into Them.* When you keep giving
others what nobody else will, they will return to
your life.

42. *Sow Into Others What Others Are
Incapable Of Sowing—Time, Kindness And Love.*
Few will intercede for your son or daughter. Your
Seed of Intercession will produce a Harvest nobody
else can produce in their life.

43. *Sow That Which Is Eternal, And You Will
Create An Eternal Bond Of Loyalty With Others.*
They will celebrate you for a lifetime. Most ministers recognize that people who come to Christ
under their ministry have a different loyalty and
feeling toward them than anyone else.

44. *Sow Without Complaining About It.*
Unthankfulness is deadly and can destroy the
effect of every good Seed.

45. *Your Seed Is The Vehicle Into Your
Future.*

46. *Your Seed Is The Only Influence You Have Over Your Future.*

47. *Your Seed Is A Weapon Against Greed, Fear And Unbelief.*

48. *Your Seed Forces The Future To Whimper At Your Feet Like A Puppy, Begging For An Instruction.*

49. *The Seed Of Forgiveness Unleashes One Thousand Time More Mercy Back To You.* It makes relationships possible. God becomes involved with those who let their forgiveness flow through them like Seeds.

50. *The Seed Of Love Unleashes One Thousand Times More Love Around You In Crisis.*

51. *The Seed Of Excellence Gets One Thousand Times Higher Excellence Around You.* This is revealed when you put quality into every word you say, the tasks you complete and your boss can know that no one can do it better than you.

52. *The Seed Of Diligence Can Unleash One Thousand Times More Favor With The King And Leaders Of Your World.* This is immediate attention to the priorities and focus of those in authority over you.

53. *The Seed Of Favor Launches One Thousand Times More Favor Toward You.* One Day Of Favor Is Worth A Thousand Days Of Labor. You cannot expect it to come until you have planted it like a Seed into the lives of others.

54. *The Seed Of Time Into Those You Love Can Unleash One Thousand Times More Love.* Whatever You Give Time Toward Is Proof Of What You Value The Most In Life.

55. *The Seed Of Finances Can Unleash One Thousand Times More Provision.* Money is the god of this world. That is why the money Seed is more powerful than any other Seed you could plant. When you plant a money Seed, you have given *all* of you.

It takes all you *know* to earn your money. So, when you bring a money Seed to God, you are bringing Him the best of your *Intelligence.*

It takes every *relationship* in your life to create money flow. So, when you bring an offering to God, you are bringing Him the cream and the best of your *Relationships.*

It takes the best *hours* of your day to create your paycheck. So, when you bring God an offering, you are bringing Him the best of your *Time.*

It takes your *health* and *energy* to create finances and solve problems. So, when you bring God an offering, you are bringing Him your very *body.*

That is the phenomenon of sowing Seeds into the work of God.

Sow Uncommon Seeds Expectantly...and you will see the One Thousand Times More promise come to pass in your life.

56. *Sow What You Have Been Given.* Stop complaining about something you do not have. You lack money? Then, use your time as a Seed. Work for your boss, the local church, or simply baby-sit for someone who is overworked. Use your time as arrows and Seeds.

57. *You Must Sow Whatever You Presently Have.* Do not wait until "my ship comes in." Begin

now. Small Seeds set big miracles in motion.

58. *Sow Habitually.* Consecutive sowing creates consistent reaping. If you sow erratically, you will reap erratically.

59. *Wrap Your Faith Around Your Seed When You Sow.* Your Seed is *what* God multiplies; but, your faith is *why* He multiplies it.

60. *Speak Expectation Into Your Seed.* The only pain God knows is to be doubted. His only pleasure is to be believed. Expectation effects the events of your life greatly.

"But without faith it is impossible to please Him; for he that cometh to God must believe that He is, and that He is a rewarder of them that diligently seek Him" (Hebrews 11:6).

Many were blind and sick during the days of Jesus. But, the blind man that cried out with great expectation...experienced his miracle!

61. *Your Words Are Revealing Your Expectations.* Stop talking doubt. Stop discussing every success of satan. Never Say Anything That Makes Your Enemies Think They Are Winning.

62. *What You Are Talking About The Most Is Revealing What You Are Expecting In Your Life.* Walk toward a restaurant table and look and observe the excitement on the countenances! A young mother-to-be is excited. Everybody is listening to her! Why? She is talking about her *expectation*...her newborn child about to enter her life. Everyone discusses their expectations.

63. *What You Are Talking About The Most Is Beginning To Increase In Your Life.* Your mouth is a Multiplier. "Death and life are in the power of

the tongue: and they that love it shall eat the fruit thereof" (Proverbs 18:21). "For by thy words thou shalt be justified, and by thy words thou shalt be condemned" (Matthew 12:37).

64. *What You Are Thinking About The Most, Your Body Is Moving Toward.* Picture yourself watching television. Suddenly a commercial comes on about hamburgers. Then, fried chicken. Within seconds, you have walked into the kitchen and began to browse through the refrigerator. Why? What Happens In Your Mind Begins To Happen In Your Life. Your body will follow the desires of your mind.

65. *Expect The Impossible And The Impossible Will Move Quickly Toward You.* "For verily I say unto you, That whosoever shall say unto this mountain, Be thou removed, and be thou cast into the sea; and shall not doubt in his heart, but shall believe that those things which he saith shall come to pass; he shall have whatsoever he saith" (Mark 11:23).

66. *Never Debate With The Holy Spirit About A Seed He Is Instructing You To Sow.* Do not cause Him to withdraw from you. Faith attracts Him. Faith excites Him. Expectation is His pleasure. Do not rob Him of that special moment of obedience that brings the only pleasure He knows.

67. *Sow Your Seed In Complete Obedience To The Voice Of The Holy Spirit...With Expectation.*

68. *Sow With Expectation Of A 1,000-Fold Return.* Deuteronomy 1:11 is not a Dream. It is a fact. God wants you to become *One Thousand Times More* than you have ever been. He wants to show His power through your life.

69. *The Seed That Would Leave My Hand Would Never Leave My Life—Just My Hand, And Enter Into My Future Where It Would Multiply!*

70. *When God Talks To You About A Seed, He Has A Harvest On His Mind.*

71. *An Uncommon Seed Always Creates An Uncommon Harvest.*

How I Broke The Back Of Poverty In My Life!

I *broke the back of poverty* with an Uncommon Seed. A Seed of $1,000. I will never forget it as long as I live. It happened on a telethon. I had just received an incredible royalty check for my song writing of $5,000. I was ecstatic! You see, I did not have anything. Sheets were tacked over my windows. I wanted draperies so bad. I needed a kitchen table with chairs. I had *nothing!* So, I really had wonderful plans for my $5,000! It was my Harvest!

Suddenly, the Holy Spirit spoke to me while sitting next to some ministers on the telethon.

"I want you to plant a Seed of $1,000."

Well, I explained to the Holy Spirit, that I was going to buy draperies and a kitchen table with chairs! (It took Him over 45 minutes before I fully obeyed Him.)

The next day, He spoke again. I planted a *second* Seed of $1,000 as a Covenant for my son, Jason. Then the following Sunday morning, the Holy Spirit spoke to me the *third* time to plant a third Seed of $1,000 at a church in Dallas. That afternoon cannot be explained or described adequately! I was in torment and ecstasy at the same time. I felt a little sick inside because I felt like I had gotten "carried away." I knelt at the pastor's little office that afternoon before service. My heart was quite troubled.

"Holy Spirit, five days ago I had $5,000. Within the last five days, You have spoken to me to plant three Seeds of $1,000. If this is not You and Your plan, stop me now!"

The Holy Spirit explained to me that *when He talked to me about a Seed, He had a Harvest on His mind.* When I opened my hand, He would open His windows. The Seed that would leave my hand would never leave my life—just my hand, and enter into my future where it would multiply!

The miracles began.

That night after the Sunday night service, a man walked up. He opened a book featuring rare automobiles. He explained one of the cars in it and said, "There's only 19 of these in the world. I happen to have Serial Number 1—the first one they made. It is my pet car. *God told me to give it to you!*"

The next day, Monday morning, a man walked into my office. He said, "I understand you need a van for your ministry? Order the best one you can buy, and *I'll pay for it.*"

Tuesday morning, the next day, a brother called me for lunch. As we sat at the restaurant, he explained that he could not sleep that night. The Holy Spirit kept speaking to him to give me a special Seed of $10,000!

My life has never been the same.

Within a couple of years, almost $400,000 came into my pocket and life from song-writing royalties. It was astounding.

When God Talks To You About A Seed, He Has A Harvest On His Mind.

Get your faith up!!

Your Personal Checklist For Increase

▶ God Even Commanded Adam And Eve To Be Fruitful And Multiply And Have Dominion. "And God blessed them, and God said unto them, Be fruitful, and multiply, and replenish the earth, and subdue it: and have dominion over the fish of the sea, and over the fowl of the air, and over every living thing that moveth upon the earth" (Genesis 1:28).

▶ God Commanded Every Living Thing To Multiply. "And God blessed them, saying, Be fruitful, and multiply, and fill the waters in the seas, and let fowl multiply in the earth" (Genesis 1:22).

▶ God Guaranteed That The Principle Of Increase Would Operate As Long As The Earth Existed. "While the earth remaineth, seedtime and harvest, and cold and heat, and summer and winter, and day and night shall not cease" (Genesis 8:22).

▶ God Wants To Be The Source Of Your Increase. "If ye then, being evil, know how to give good gifts unto your children, how much more shall your Father which

is in heaven give good things to them
that ask Him?" (Matthew 7:11).

Review this checklist for increasing your
Harvest. Remember, Every Harvest Requires A
Seed.

□ 1. *God Wants To Increase The Miracles You
Experience.* "For verily I say unto you, That whosoever shall say unto this mountain, Be thou
removed, and be thou cast into the sea; and shall
not doubt in his heart, but shall believe that those
things which he saith shall come to pass; he shall
have whatsoever he saith. Therefore I say unto
you, What things soever ye desire, when ye pray,
believe that ye receive them, and ye shall have
them" (Mark 11:23,24).

□ 2. *God Wants To Increase The Rejoicing Of
Your Life.* "Make a joyful noise unto the Lord, all
the earth: make a loud noise, and rejoice, and sing
praise" (Psalm 98:4).

□ 3. *God Wants To Increase Your Worship To
Him.* "Sing unto the Lord with the harp; with the
harp, and the voice of a psalm. With trumpets and
sound of cornet make a joyful noise before the
Lord, the King" (Psalm 98:5,6).

□ 4. *God Wants To Increase Revelation In Your
Life.* Rewards are inevitable and remarkable.
"What man is he that feareth the Lord? Him shall
He teach in the way that He shall choose. His soul
shall dwell at ease; and his seed shall inherit the
earth. The secret of the Lord is with them that fear
Him; and He will shew them His covenant" (Psalm
25:12-14).

□ 5. *God Wants To Increase Your Wisdom.* "If
any of you lack wisdom, let him ask of God, that

giveth to all men liberally, and upbraideth not; and it shall be given him" (James 1:5). "Wherein He hath abounded toward us in all wisdom and prudence;" (Ephesians 1:8).

☐ 6. *God Wants To Increase Your Finances.* "Blessed is the man that feareth the Lord,...Wealth and riches shall be in his house: and his righteousness endureth for ever" (Psalm 112:1,3).

☐ 7. *God Wants To Increase Your Life Span On The Earth.* "Honour thy father and mother; (which is the first commandment with promise;) That it may be well with thee, and thou mayest live long on the earth" (Ephesians 6:2,3).

"They shall still bring forth fruit in old age; they shall be fat and flourishing;" (Psalm 92:14).

☐ 8. *God Wants You To Increase In Maturity.* "But speaking the truth in love, may grow up into Him in all things, which is the head, even Christ:" (Ephesians 4:15).

☐ 9. *God Wants You To Increase In Grace.* "But grow in grace, and in the knowledge of our Lord and Saviour Jesus Christ" (2 Peter 3:18).

☐ 10. *God Wants You To Increase In Purity.* "If we confess our sins, He is faithful and just to forgive us our sins, and to cleanse us from all unrighteousness" (1 John 1:9).

☐ 11. *God Wants Your Life To Increase In Love.* "But whoso keepeth His Word, in him verily is the love of God perfected: hereby know we that we are in Him" (1 John 2:5). "...because the love of God is shed abroad in our hearts by the Holy Ghost which is given unto us" (Romans 5:5).

☐ 12. *God Wants You To Increase In Joy.* "These things have I spoken unto you, that My joy might remain in you, and that your joy might be full. This is My commandment, That ye love one another, as I have loved you" (John 15:11,12).

☐ 13. *The Holy Spirit Will Bring An Increase Of Truth In You.* "Howbeit when He, the Spirit of Truth, is come, He will guide you into all truth: for He shall not speak of Himself; but whatsoever He shall hear, that shall He speak: and He will shew you things to come" (John 16:13).

☐ 14. *God Wants You To Increase In Humility.* "Let nothing be done through strife or vainglory; but in lowliness of mind let each esteem other better than themselves" (Philippians 2:3).

☐ 15. *God Wants You To Increase In The Fruit You Produce.* "That ye might walk worthy of the Lord unto all pleasing, being fruitful in every good work, and increasing in the knowledge of God;" (Colossians 1:10).

☐ 16. *God Wants You To Increase In Strength.* "Strengthened with all might, according to His glorious power, unto all patience and longsuffering with joyfulness;" (Colossians 1:11).

☐ 17. *God Wants You To Increase In Obedience.* "Now therefore, if ye will obey My voice indeed, and keep My covenant, then ye shall be a peculiar treasure unto Me above all people: for all the earth is Mine:" (Exodus 19:5).

☐ 18. *God Wants To Increase The Flow Of Blessings Into Your Life.* "And it shall come to pass, if thou shalt hearken diligently unto the voice of the Lord thy God, to observe and to do all His commandments which I command thee this day, that the Lord thy God will set thee on high above all nations of the earth: And all these blessings shall come on thee, and overtake thee, if thou shalt hearken unto the voice of the Lord thy God" (Deuteronomy 28:1,2).

☐ 19. *God Wants You To Increase Your Victories Over Your Enemies.* "The Lord shall cause thine enemies that rise up against thee to be smitten before thy face: they shall come out against thee one way, and flee before thee seven ways" (Deuteronomy 28:7).

☐ 20. *God Wants His Word To Increase In You.* "And the Word of God increased; and the number of disciples multiplied in Jerusalem greatly; and a great company of the priests were obedient to the faith" (Acts 6:7).

☐ 21. *God Wants Your Endurance Ability To Increase.* After the disciples were beaten, the Bible says, "And they departed from the presence of the council, rejoicing that they were counted worthy to suffer shame for His name" (Acts 5:41).

☐ 22. *God Wants Your Peace To Increase.* "And the peace of God, which passeth all understanding, shall keep your hearts and minds through Christ Jesus" (Philippians 4:7).

☐ 23. *God Wants Your Thoughts To Increase In Purity And Truth.* "Finally, brethren, whatsoever things are true, whatsoever things are honest, whatsoever things are just, whatsoever things are pure, whatsoever things are lovely, whatsoever things are of good report; if there be any virtue, and if there by any praise, think on these things" (Philippians 4:8).

☐ 24. *God Wants Your Thanksgiving And Praise To Increase.* "In every thing give thanks: for this is the will of God in Christ Jesus concerning you" (1 Thessalonians 5:18).

☐ 25. *God Wants Your Prayer Life To Increase.* "Pray without ceasing" (1 Thessalonians 5:17).

☐ 26. *God Wants Your Ability To Fast To Increase.* "Is not this the fast that I have chosen? to loose the bands of wickedness, to undo the heavy burdens, and to let the oppressed go free, and that ye break every yoke?" (Isaiah 58:6).

☐ 27. *God Wants Your Health And Healing To Increase.* "Then shall thy light break forth as the morning, and thine health shall spring forth speedily:" (Isaiah 58:8).

☐ 28. *God Wants Your Soul Winning To Increase.* "Go ye into all the world, and preach the gospel to every creature" (Mark 16:15). "He that winneth souls is wise" (Proverbs 11:30).

☐ 29. *God Wants You To Increase Your Giving To The Poor.* "He that giveth unto the poor shall not lack: but he that hideth his eyes shall have many a curse" (Proverbs 28:27; also see Proverbs 11:24-26.)

☐ 30. *God Wants To Increase The Size Of Your Church.* "And the Lord added to the church daily such as should be saved" (Acts 2:47). "And the word of God increased; and the number of disciples multiplied in Jerusalem greatly; and a great company of the priests were obedient to the faith" (Acts 6:7).

☐ 31. *God Wants To Increase The Flow Of Favor In Your Life.* "For Thou, Lord, wilt bless the righteous; with favour wilt Thou compass him as with a shield" (Psalm 5:12).

☐ 32. *God Wants To Increase The Shouting And Laughter In Your Life.* "Make a joyful noise unto the Lord, all the earth: make a loud noise, and rejoice, and sing praise" (Psalm 98:4).

☐ 33. *God Wants To Increase Your Singing To Him.* "Sing unto the Lord with the harp; with the harp, and the voice of a psalm. With trumpets and sound of cornet make a joyful noise before the Lord, the King" (Psalm 98:5,6).

☐ 34. *God Wants To Increase Protection Around You.* "There shall no evil befall thee, neither shall any plague come nigh thy dwelling. For He shall give His angels charge over thee, to keep thee in all thy ways" (Psalm 91:10,11).

☐ 35. *God Wants To Increase His Mercies In Your Life.* "It is of the Lord's mercies that we are not consumed, because His compassions fail not. They are new every morning: great is Thy faithfulness" (Lamentations 3:22,23).

☐ 36. *God Wants To Increase The Patience In Your Life.* "The Lord is good unto them that wait for Him, to the soul that seeketh Him. It is good that a man should both hope and quietly wait for the salvation of the Lord" (Lamentations 3:25,26).

☐ 37. *God Wants To Increase His Achievements Through Your Life.* "Now unto Him that is able to do exceeding abundantly above all that we ask or think, according to the power that worketh in us," (Ephesians 3:20).

☐ 38. *God Wants To Increase His Power In Your Own Life.* "But ye shall receive power, after that the Holy Ghost is come upon you:" (Acts 1:8).

☐ 39. *God Wants To Increase Your Pleasure In His World.* "They shall be abundantly satisfied with the fatness of Thy house; and Thou shalt make them drink of the river of Thy pleasures. For with Thee is the fountain of life: in Thy light shall we see light" (Psalm 36:8,9).

☐ 40. *God Wants To Increase The Rest In Your Life.* "Rest in the Lord, and wait patiently for Him: fret not thyself because of him who prospereth in his way, because of the man who bringeth wicked devices to pass" (Psalm 37:7).

☐ 41. *God Wants The Fear Of The Lord To Increase In Your Life.* "The fear of the Lord is the beginning of wisdom: and the knowledge of the Holy is understanding" (Proverbs 9:10).

☐ 42. *God Wants To Increase The Good That You Do For Others.* "Withhold not good from them to whom it is due, when it is in the power of thine hand to do it" (Proverbs 3:27).

☐ 43. *God Wants To Increase The Self-Confidence Within You Toward His Assignment In Your Life.* "Be not afraid of sudden fear, neither the desolation of the wicked, when it cometh. For the Lord shall be thy confidence, and shall keep thy foot from being taken" (Proverbs 3:25,26).

☐ 44. *God Even Desires To Increase The Sweetness Of Your Sleep At Night.* "When thou liest down, thou shalt not be afraid: yea, thou shalt lie down, and thy sleep shall be sweet" (Proverbs 3:24). "And I will give peace in the land, and ye shall lie down, and none shall make you afraid:" (Leviticus 26:6).

☐ 45. *God Wants To Increase The Time You Fellowship With Him.* "And I will walk among you, and will be your God, and ye shall be My people" (Leviticus 26:12).

☐ 46. *God Wants To Increase The Time You Invest In Your Own Personal Secret Place.* "One thing have I desired of the Lord, that will I seek after; that I may dwell in the house of the Lord all the days of my life, to behold the beauty of the Lord, and to inquire in His temple" (Psalm 27:4).

☐ 47. *God Wants To Increase Your Personal Integrity.* "Let integrity and uprightness preserve me; for I wait on Thee" (Psalm 25:21).

☐ 48. *God Wants To Increase What The Whole Earth Produces For You.* "If ye walk in My statutes, and keep My commandments, and do them; Then I will give you rain in due season, and the land shall yield her increase, and the trees of the field shall yield their fruit. And your threshing shall reach unto the vintage, and the vintage shall reach unto the sowing time: and ye shall eat your bread to the full, and dwell in your land safely" (Leviticus 26:3-5).

☐ 49. *God Wants To Increase Your Sowing So Your Reaping Can Increase.* "He which soweth sparingly shall reap also sparingly; and he which soweth bountifully shall reap also bountifully" (2 Corinthians 9:6).

☐ 50. *God Wants To Increase Compensation For Every Loss You Experience Because Of Him.* "And Jesus answered and said, Verily I say unto you, There is no man that hath left house, or brethren, or sisters, or father, or mother, or wife, or children, or lands, for My sake, and the gospel's, But he shall receive an hundredfold now in this time, houses, and brethren, and sisters, and mothers, and children, and lands, with persecutions; and in the world to come eternal life" (Mark 10:29,30).

☐ 51. *God Wants To Increase The Forgiveness You Receive From Others.* "Give, and it shall be given unto you; good measure, pressed down, and shaken together, and running over, shall men give into your bosom. For with the same measure that ye mete withal it shall be measured to you again" (Luke 6:38).

☐ 52.   *God Wants To Increase The Church, The Body Of Christ, One Thousand Times More.* Yes, it is impossible to doubt this Principle of Blessing— God wants to increase you. "And He increased His people greatly; and made them stronger than their enemies" (Psalm 105:24).

Our Prayer Together...

"Holy Spirit, You have directed my steps in the writing of this book. You have poured incredible strength, energy and revelation into my heart for my special friend today. Ignite these pages. Unleash the fire from the altars of Heaven into our heart and mind today. Set our faith on fire. Annihilate any cobweb of unbelief from every corner of our life. You are the God of increase, the God of multiplication and miracles.

I enter into a Covenant for the promise of *One Thousand Times More* and I am not coming out of this agreement until the Harvest arrives.

In the name of Jesus, the Best Seed You ever planted. Amen."

31 WISDOM KEYS THAT MOST CHANGED MY LIFE

1. Never Complain About What You Permit.
2. What You Respect Will Come Toward You.
3. The Problem That Infuriates You The Most Is The Problem God Has Assigned You To Solve.
4. The Secret Of Your Future Is Hidden In Your Daily Routine.
5. What You Are Willing To Move Away From Determines What God Will Bring To You.
6. Your Rewards In Life Are Determined By The Problems You Solve For Others.
7. You Will Only Have Significant Success When Your Assignment Becomes An Obsession.
8. You Will Never Possess What You Are Unwilling To Pursue.
9. Champions Are Willing To Do Things They Hate To Create Something They Love.
10. The Only Reason Men Fail Is Broken Focus.
11. Those Who Sin With You Will Eventually Sin Against You.
12. False Accusation Is The Last Stage Before Supernatural Promotion.
13. Your Significance Is Not In Your Similarity To Another, But In Your Point Of Difference From Another.
14. What You Fail To Conquer In Your Life Will Eventually Conquer You.

15. When You Let Go Of What Is In Your Hand, God Will Let Go Of What Is In His Hand.
16. Your Reaction To A Man Of God Determines God's Reaction To You.
17. Patience Is The Weapon That Forces Deception To Reveal Itself.
18. When God Wants To Bless You, He Removes Someone From Your Life.
19. God Never Consults Your Past To Determine Your Future.
20. Pain Is The Proof Of Disorder.
21. An Uncommon Seed Always Produces An Uncommon Harvest.
22. Whatever You Have Been Given Will Create Anything Else You Have Been Promised.
23. One Day Of Favor Is Worth A Thousand Days Of Labor.
24. The Size Of Your Enemy Determines The Size Of Your Reward.
25. You Will Only Be Remembered For The Problems You Solve Or The Ones You Create.
26. Nothing Is Ever As Bad As It First Appears.
27. Seed-Faith Is Sowing What You Have Been Given To Create Something Else You Have Been Promised.
28. What You Do Daily Is Deciding What You Become Permanently.
29. The Only Difference Between Your Present And Your Future Is Your Wisdom.
30. What You Make Happen For Others, God Will Make Happen For You.
31. When You Want Something You Have Never Had, You Have Got To Do Something You Have Never Done.

Reading The Bible In One Year: A Complete Program

January

1.	Gen. 1-3	9.	Gen. 27-29	17.	Ex. 3-5	25.	Ex. 29-33
2.	Gen. 4-6	10.	Gen. 30-32	18.	Ex. 6-10	26.	Ex. 34-36
3.	Gen. 7-9	11.	Gen. 33-37	19.	Ex. 11-13	27.	Ex. 37-39
4.	Gen. 10-14	12.	Gen. 38-40	20.	Ex. 14-16	28.	Ex. 40-
5.	Gen. 15-17	13.	Gen. 41-43	21.	Ex. 17-19		Lev. 1-2
6.	Gen. 18-20	14.	Gen. 44-46	22.	Ex. 20-22	29.	Lev. 3-5
7.	Gen. 21-23	15.	Gen. 47-49	23.	Ex. 23-25	30.	Lev. 6-8
8.	Gen. 24-26	16.	Gen. 50-	24.	Ex. 26-28	31.	Lev. 9-11
			Ex.1-2				

February

1.	Lev. 12-16	7.	Num. 5-7	15.	Num. 31-35	22.	Dt. 18-22
2.	Lev. 17-19	8.	Num. 8-12	16.	Num. 36-	23.	Dt. 23-25
3.	Lev. 20-22	9.	Num. 13-15		Dt. 1-2	24.	Dt. 26-28
4.	Lev. 23-25	10.	Num. 16-18	17.	Dt. 3-5	25.	Dt. 29-31
5.	Lev. 26-27-	11.	Num. 19-21	18.	Dt. 6-8	26.	Dt. 32-34
	Num. 1	12.	Num. 22-24	19.	Dt. 9-11	27.	Josh. 1-3
6.	Num. 2-4	13.	Num. 25-27	20.	Dt. 12-14	28.	Josh. 4-6
		14.	Num. 28-30	21.	Dt. 15-17		

March

1.	Josh. 7-11	8.	Judg. 6-10	16.	1 Sam. 9-11	25.	2 Sam. 7-9
2.	Josh. 12-14	9.	Judg. 11-13	17.	1 Sam. 12-14	26.	2 Sam. 10-12
3.	Josh. 15-17	10.	Judg. 14-16	18.	1 Sam. 15-17	27.	2 Sam. 13-15
4.	Josh. 18-20	11.	Judg. 17-19	19.	1 Sam. 18-20	28.	2 Sam. 16-18
5.	Josh. 21-23	12.	Judg. 20-21-	20.	1 Sam. 21-23	29.	2 Sam. 19-23
6.	Josh. 24-		Ruth 1	21.	1 Sam. 24-26	30.	2 Sam. 24-
	Judg. 1-2	13.	Ruth 2-4	22.	1 Sam. 27-31		1 Ki. 1-2
7.	Judg. 3-5	14.	1 Sam. 1-3	23.	2 Sam. 1-3	31.	1 Ki. 3-5
		15.	1 Sam. 4-8	24.	2 Sam. 4-6		

April

1.	1 Ki. 6-8	9.	2 Ki. 10-12	16.	1 Chr. 8-10	23.	2 Chr. 2-4
2.	1 Ki. 9-11	10.	2 Ki. 13-15	17.	1 Chr. 11-13	24.	2 Chr. 5-7
3.	1 Ki. 12-14	11.	2 Ki. 16-18	18.	1 Chr. 14-16	25.	2 Chr. 8-10
4.	1 Ki. 15-17	12.	2 Ki. 19-23	19.	1 Chr. 17-21	26.	2 Chr. 11-15
5.	1 Ki. 18-22	13.	2 Ki. 24-25-	20.	1 Chr. 22-24	27.	2 Chr. 16-18
6.	2 Ki. 1-3		1 Chr. 1	21.	1 Chr. 25-27	28.	2 Chr. 19-21
7.	2 Ki. 4-6	14.	1 Chr. 2-4	22.	1 Chr. 28-	29.	2 Chr. 22-24
8.	2 Ki. 7-9	15.	1 Chr. 5-7		29-2 Chr. 1	30.	2 Chr. 25-27

MAY

1.	2 Chr. 28-30	8.	Neh. 5-7	15.	Job 5-7	24.	Job 34-38
2.	2 Chr. 31-33	9.	Neh. 8-10	16.	Job. 8-10	25.	Job 39-41
3.	2 Chr. 34-36-Ez.1-2	10.	Neh. 11-13-Esth. 1-2	17.	Job 11-15	26.	Job 42-Ps.1-2
4.	Ez. 3-5	11.	Esth. 3-5	18.	Job 16-18	27.	Ps. 3-5
5.	Ez. 6-8	12.	Esth. 6-8	19.	Job 19-21	28.	Ps. 6-8
6.	Ez. 9-10-Neh. 1	13.	Esth. 9-10-Job 1	20.	Job 22-24	29.	Ps. 9-11
7.	Neh. 2-4	14.	Job 2-4	21.	Job 25-27	30.	Ps. 12-14
				22.	Job 28-30	31.	Ps. 15-19
				23.	Job 31-33		

JUNE

1.	Ps. 20-22	8.	Ps. 43-45	16.	Ps. 69-71	24.	Ps. 95-97
2.	Ps. 23-25	9.	Ps. 46-48	17.	Ps. 72-74	25.	Ps. 98-100
3.	Ps. 26-28	10.	Ps. 49-51	18.	Ps. 75-77	26.	Ps. 101-103
4.	Ps. 29-31	11.	Ps. 52-54	19.	Ps. 78-80	27.	Ps. 104-106
5.	Ps. 32-34	12.	Ps. 55-57	20.	Ps. 81-83	28.	Ps. 107-111
6.	Ps. 35-37	13.	Ps. 58-60	21.	Ps. 84-88	29.	Ps. 112-114
7.	Ps. 38-42	14.	Ps. 61-65	22.	Ps. 89-91	30.	Ps. 115-117
		15.	Ps. 66-68	23.	Ps. 92-94		

JULY

1.	Ps. 118-120	10.	Ps. 147-149	18.	Prov. 23-25	25.	SoS. 3-5
2.	Ps. 121-123	11.	Ps. 150-Prov. 1-2	19.	Prov. 26-30	26.	SoS. 6-8-Is. 1-2
3.	Ps. 124-126			20.	Prov. 31-Ecc. 1-2	27.	Is. 3-5
4.	Ps. 127-129	12.	Prov. 3-7	21.	Ecc. 3-5	28.	Is. 6-8
5.	Ps. 130-134	13.	Prov. 8-10	22.	Ecc. 6-8	29.	Is. 9-11
6.	Ps. 135-137	14.	Prov. 11-13	23.	Ecc. 9-11	30.	Is. 12-14
7.	Ps. 138-140	15.	Prov. 14-16	24.	Ecc. 12-SoS. 1-2	31.	Is. 15-17
8.	Ps. 141-143	16.	Prov. 17-19				
9.	Ps. 144-146	17.	Prov. 20-22				

AUGUST

1.	Is. 18-20	9.	Is. 44-48	17.	Jer. 6-8	25.	Jer. 32-34
2.	Is. 21-25	10.	Is. 49-51	18.	Jer. 9-11	26.	Jer. 35-37
3.	Is. 26-28	11.	Is. 52-54	19.	Jer. 12-14	27.	Jer. 38-40
4.	Is. 29-31	12.	Is. 55-57	20.	Jer. 15-17	28.	Jer. 41-43
5.	Is. 32-34	13.	Is. 58-60	21.	Jer. 18-20	29.	Jer. 44-46
6.	Is. 35-37	14.	Is. 61-63	22.	Jer. 21-23	30.	Jer. 47-51
7.	Is. 38-40	15.	Is. 64-66	23.	Jer. 24-28	31.	Jer. 52-Lam. 1-2
8.	Is. 41-43	16.	Jer. 1-5	24.	Jer. 29-31		

SEPTEMBER

1. Lam. 3-5	10. Ezk. 27-29	18. Dan. 5-7	25. Joel 2-3-
2. Ezk. 1-3	11. Ezk. 30-32	19. Dan. 8-10	Amos 1
3. Ezk. 4-6	12. Ezk. 33-35	20. Dan. 11-12-	26. Amos 2-4
4. Ezk. 7-9	13. Ezk. 36-40	Hos. 1-3	27. Amos 5-9
5. Ezk. 10-12	14. Ezk. 41-43	21. Hos. 4-6	28. Ob.1-Jon. 1-2
6. Ezk. 13-17	15. Ezk. 44-46	22. Hos. 7-9	29. Jon. 3-4-
7. Ezk. 18-20	16. Ezk. 47-48-	23. Hos. 10-12	Mic. 1
8. Ezk. 21-23	Dan. 1	24. Hos. 13-14-	30. Mic. 2-4
9. Ezk. 24-26	17. Dan. 2-4	Joel 1	

OCTOBER

1. Mic. 5-7	9 Zech. 13-14-	17. Matt. 21-23	25. Lk. 3-7
2. Nah. 1-3	Mal. 1	18. Matt. 24-28	26. Lk. 8-10
3. Hab. 1-3	10. Mal. 2-4	19. Mk. 1-3	27. Lk. 11-13
4. Zeph. 1-3-	11. Matt. 1-5	20. Mk. 4-6	28. Lk. 14-16
Hag. 1-2	12. Matt. 6-8	21. Mk. 7-9	29. Lk. 17-19
5. Zech. 1-3	13. Matt. 9-11	22. Mk. 10-12	30. Lk. 20-22
6. Zech. 4-6	14. Matt. 12-14	23. Mk. 13-15	31. Lk.23-24-
7. Zech. 7-9	15. Matt. 15-17	24. Mk. 16-	Jn. 1
8. Zech. 10-12	16. Matt. 18-20	Lk. 1-2	

NOVEMBER

1. Jn. 2-6	9. Acts 9-11	17. Rom. 7-9	25. 2 Cor. 1-3
2. Jn. 7-9	10. Acts 12-14	18. Rom. 10-12	26. 2 Cor. 4-6
3. Jn. 10-12	11. Acts 15-17	19. Rom. 13-15	27. 2 Cor. 7-9
4. Jn. 13-15	12. Acts 18-20	20. Rom. 16-	28. 2 Cor. 10-12
5. Jn. 16-18	13. Acts 21-23	1 Cor. 1-2	29. 2 Cor. 13-
6. Jn. 19-21	14. Acts 24-26	21. 1 Cor. 3-5	Gal. 1-4
7. Acts 1-3	15. Acts 27-28-	22. 1 Cor. 6-10	30. Gal. 5-6-
8. Acts 4-8	Rom. 1-3	23. 1 Cor. 11-13	Eph. 1
	16. Rom. 4-6	24. 1 Cor. 14-16	

DECEMBER

1. Eph. 2-4	8. 1 Tim. 3-5	15. Heb. 12-13-	22. Rev. 1-3
2. Eph. 5-6-	9. 1 Tim. 6-	James 1	23. Rev. 4-5
Ph. 1	2 Tim. 1-2	16. James 2-4	24. Rev. 6-7
3. Ph. 2-4	10. 2 Tim. 3-4-	17. James 5-	25. Rev. 8-9
4. Col. 1-3	Tit. 1	1 Peter 1-2	26. Rev. 10-11
5. Col. 4-	11. Tit. 2-3-	18. 1 Peter 3-5	27. Rev. 12-16
1 Thes.1-2	Phil. 1	19. 2 Peter 1-3	28. Rev. 17-18
6. 1 Thes. 3-5-	12. Heb. 1-3	20. 1 Jn. 1-5	29. Rev. 19-20
2 Thes. 1-2	13. Heb. 4-8	21. 2 Jn. 1-3 Jn.	30. Rev. 21-22
7. 2 Thes. 3-	14. Heb. 9-11	1-Jude 1	31. Well Done!
1 Tim. 1-2			

JOIN THE
Wisdom Key 3000
TODAY!

Dear Partner,

God has connected us!

I have asked the Holy Spirit for 3000 Special Partners who will plant a monthly Seed of $58.00 to help me bring the gospel around the world. (58 represents 58 kinds of blessing in the Bible.)

Will you become my monthly Faith Partner in The Wisdom Key 3000? Your monthly Seed of $58.00 is so powerful in helping heal broken lives. When you sow into the work of God, 4 Miracle Harvests are guaranteed in Scripture:

- ► Uncommon Protection (Mal. 3:10,11)
- ► Uncommon Favor (Lk. 6:38)
- ► Uncommon Health (Isa. 58:8)
- ► Financial Ideas and Wisdom (Deut. 8:18)

Your Faith Partner,

Mike Murdock

☐ **Yes Mike, I want to join The Wisdom Key 3000. Enclosed is my monthly Seed-Faith Promise of ☐ $58 ☐ Other $_____. Please rush The Wisdom Key Partnership Pak to me today!**

☐ MONEY ORDER ☐ CHECK ☐ VISA ☐ MASTERCARD ☐ AMEX ☐ DISCOVER

Credit Card # _____ Exp. ____/____

Signature _____

Name _____ Birth Date ____/____/____

Address _____

City _____ State _____ Zip _____

Phone _____ E-Mail _____

Your Seed-Faith offerings are used to support the Mike Murdock Evangelistic Association, The Wisdom Center and all its programs. The Ministry reserves the right to redirect funds as needed in order to carry out our charitable purpose.

Clip and mail completed form to:

THE WISDOM CENTER
P.O. Box 99, Denton, Texas 76202

1-888-WISDOM1
(1-888-947-3661)

Website:
WWW.THEWISDOMCENTER.TV

DECISION

Will You Accept Jesus As Your Personal Savior Today?

The Bible says, "That if thou shalt confess with thy mouth the Lord Jesus, and shalt believe in thine heart that God hath raised Him from the dead, thou shalt be saved" (Romans 10:9).

Pray this prayer from your heart today!

"Dear Jesus, I believe that You died for me and rose again on the third day. I confess I am a sinner...I need Your love and forgiveness...Come into my heart. Forgive my sins. I receive Your eternal life. Confirm Your love by giving me peace, joy and supernatural love for others. Amen."

DR. MIKE MURDOCK is in tremendous demand as one of the most dynamic speakers in America today.

More than 14,000 audiences in 38 countries have attended his Schools of Wisdom. Hundreds of invitations come to him from churches, colleges and business corporations. He is a noted author of over 130 books, including the best sellers, *"The Leadership Secrets of Jesus"* and *"Secrets of the Richest Man Who Ever Lived."* Thousands view his weekly television program, *"Wisdom Keys with Mike Murdock."* Many attend his Saturday School of Wisdom Breakfasts that he hosts in major cities of America.

Clip and Mail

127

DR. MIKE MURDOCK

1 Has embraced his Assignment to Pursue...Proclaim...and Publish the Wisdom of God to help people achieve their dreams and goals.

2 Began full-time evangelism at the age of 19, which has continued since 1966.

3 Has traveled and spoken to more than 14,000 audiences in 38 countries, including East and West Africa, the Orient and Europe.

4 Noted author of 130 books, including best sellers, "Wisdom For Winning," "Dream Seeds" and "The Double Diamond Principle."

5 Created the popular "Topical Bible" series for Businessmen, Mothers, Fathers, Teenagers; "The One-Minute Pocket Bible" series, and "The Uncommon Life" series.

6 Has composed more than 5,700 songs such as "I Am Blessed," "You Can Make It," "God Rides On Wings Of Love" and "Jesus, Just The Mention Of Your Name," recorded by many gospel artists.

7 Is the Founder of The Wisdom Center, in Denton, Texas.

8 Has a weekly television program called *"Wisdom Keys With Mike Murdock."*

9 Has appeared often on TBN, CBN, BET and other television network programs.

10 Is a Founding Trustee on the Board of International Charismatic Bible Ministries with Oral Roberts.

11 Has had more than 3,500 accept the call into full-time ministry under his ministry.

THE MINISTRY

1 **Wisdom Books & Literature** - Over 130 best-selling Wisdom Books and 70 Teaching Tape Series.

2 **Church Crusades** - Multitudes are ministered to in crusades and seminars throughout America in "The Uncommon Wisdom Conferences." Known as a man who loves pastors he has focused on church crusades for 36 years.

3 **Music Ministry** - Millions have been blessed by the anointed songwriting and singing of Mike Murdock, who has made over 15 music albums and CDs available.

4 **Television** - *"Wisdom Keys With Mike Murdock,"* a nationally-syndicated weekly television program.

5 **The Wisdom Center** - The Ministry Offices of The Mike Murdock Evangelistic Association where Schools of Wisdom have been held.

6 **Schools of the Holy Spirit** - Mike Murdock hosts Schools of the Holy Spirit in many churches to mentor believers on the Person and Companionship of the Holy Spirit.

7 **Schools of Wisdom** - In many major cities Mike Murdock hosts Saturday Schools of Wisdom for those who want personalized and advanced training for achieving "The Uncommon Life."

8 **Missions Outreach** - Dr Mike. Murdock's overseas outreaches to 38 countries have included crusades in East and West Africa, South America, the Orient and Europe.

My Gift Of Appreciation...
The Wisdom Commentary

The Wisdom Commentary includes 52 topics...for mentoring your family every week of the year.

These topics include:

- Abilities
- Achievement
- Anointing
- Assignment
- Bitterness
- Blessing
- Career
- Change
- Children
- Dating
- Depression
- Discipline
- Divorce
- Dreams And Goals
- Enemy
- Enthusiasm
- Favor
- Finances
- Fools

- Giving
- Goal-Setting
- God
- Happiness
- Holy Spirit
- Ideas
- Intercession
- Jobs
- Loneliness
- Love
- Mentorship
- Ministers
- Miracles
- Mistakes
- Money
- Negotiation
- Prayer
- Problem-Solving
- Protégés

- Satan
- Secret Place
- Seed-Faith
- Self-Confidence
- Struggle
- Success
- Time-Management
- Understanding
- Victory
- Weaknesses
- Wisdom
- Word Of God
- Words
- Work

THE *Mike Murdock* COLLECTOR'S EDITION

The Wisdom Commentary of MIKE MURDOCK

THE WISDOM COMMENTARY 1

VOLUME 1

B-136

Gift Of Appreciation
For Your Sponsorship Seed of $100 or More
Gift Of Appreciation

My Gift Of Appreciation To My Sponsors!
...Those Who Sponsor One Square Foot In The Completion Of The Wisdom Center!

Thank you so much for becoming a part of this wonderful project...The completion of The Wisdom Center! The total purchase and renovation cost of this facility (10,000 square feet) is just over $1,000,000. This is approximately $100 per square foot. **The Wisdom Commentary is my Gift of Appreciation for your Sponsorship Seed of $100...that sponsors one square foot of The Wisdom Center. Become a Sponsor!** You will love this Volume 1, of The Wisdom Commentary. It is my exclusive Gift of Appreciation for The Wisdom Key Family who partners with me in the Work of God as a Sponsor.

Add 10% For S/H

THE WISDOM CENTER
P.O. Box 99, Denton, Texas 76202

1-888-WISDOM1
(1-888-947-3661)

Website:
WWW.THEWISDOMCENTER.TV

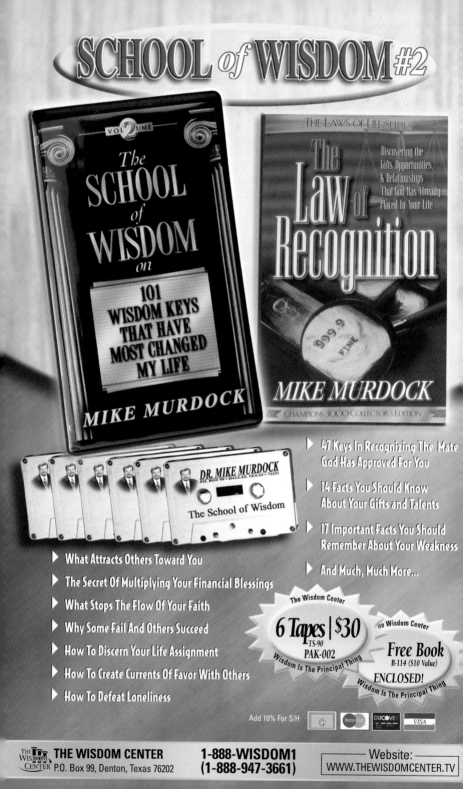

Financial Success

The Wisdom Journal

"Write The Things Which Thou Hast Seen, And The Things Which Are, And The Things Which Shall Be Hereafter."

-Revelation 1:19

Stunningly beautiful Black and Gold Leatherette. Contains 160 pages for your personal journalizing and diary...a different Wisdom Key for each day...it also includes:

► 101 Wisdom Keys
► 31 Facts About Favor
► 31 Facts About Wisdom
► 31 Facts About The Holy Spirit
► 31 Qualities Of An Unforgettable Woman
► 58 Leadership Secrets Of Jesus
► Read The Bible Through In A Year Program
► Sample Page For Effective Note Taking

The Wisdom Center

$20 Each

B-163

Wisdom Is The Principal Thing

Add 10% For S/H

THE WISDOM CENTER
P.O. Box 99, Denton, Texas 76202

1-888-WISDOM1
(1-888-947-3661)

Website:
WWW.THEWISDOMCENTER.TV

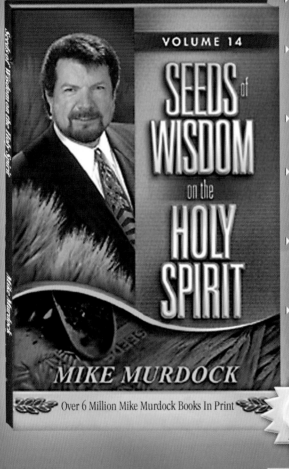

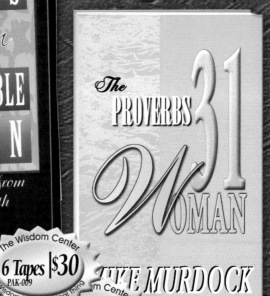

BOOK STORE

SPECIAL!

The Wisdom Center
Book Display is
available at last!

YOUR WHOLESALE PRICE

**Your price for these 445 Wisdom Books
(42 different titles) is only $1,985.00
...a 40% discount.** (Retail value of Books and
Display Stand is $3,674.00)

FREE BOOK DISPLAY

Beautiful wood grain 72" Book Rack...holding
up to 48 titles! It is a square, revolving Book
Rack with clear plastic book shelves.
The base is on casters for easy mobility...*only
18" of floor space!*

ORDER TODAY!

When you order today, The Wisdom Center
will include this splendid 72" *Book Display*
Book Rack for No Additional Cost!

WBD-72

**Shipping cost of entire
display and books
an additional...$199.00**

To place your order, contact:

THE WISDOM CENTER P.O. Box 99, Denton, Texas 76202

**1-888-WISDOM1
(1-888-947-3661)**

Website:
WWW.THEWISDOMCENTER.TV

The Wisdom Center *Book Display* (72")

THE WISDOM CENTER BOOK DISPLAY CONTAINS 445 BOOKS!

Slot #	Item #	Title Of Books	Quantity	Retail Cost Per Book	Total Retail Value
1	B-01	Wisdom For Winning	5	$10.00 ea	$50.00
2	B-01	Wisdom For Winning	5	$10.00 ea	$50.00
3	B-11	Dream Seeds	12	$9.00 ea	$108.00
4	B-26	The God Book	7	$10.00 ea	$70.00
5	B-27	The Jesus Book	7	$10.00 ea	$70.00
6	B-28	The Blessing Bible	6	$10.00 ea	$60.00
7	B-29	The Survival Bible	6	$10.00 ea	$60.00
8	B-40	Wisdom For Crisis Times	9	$9.00 ea	$81.00
9	B-42	One-Minute Businessman's Devotional	5	$12.00 ea	$60.00
10	B-43	One-Minute Businesswoman's Devotional	5	$12.00 ea	$60.00
11	B-44	31 Secrets For Career Success	9	$10.00 ea	$90.00
12	B-45	101 Wisdom Keys	17	$5.00 ea	$85.00
13	B-46	31 Facts About Wisdom	15	$5.00 ea	$75.00
14	B-47	Covenant Of Fifty-Eight Blessings	10	$8.00 ea	$80.00
15	B-48	31 Keys To A New Beginning	15	$5.00 ea	$75.00
16	B-49	The Proverbs 31 Woman	13	$7.00 ea	$91.00
17	B-54	31 Greatest Chapters In The Bible	5	$10.00 ea	$50.00
18	B-57	31 Secrets Of An Unforgettable Woman	8	$9.00 ea	$72.00
19	B-71	Wisdom: God's Golden Key To Success	11	$7.00 ea	$77.00
20	B-72	Double Diamond Daily Devotional	3	$15.00 ea	$45.00
21	B-74	The Assignment Vol. 1: The Dream And The Destiny	8	$10.00 ea	$80.00
22	B-75	The Assignment Vol. 2: The Anointing And The Adversity	7	$10.00 ea	$70.00
23	B-82	31 Reasons People Do Not Receive Their Financial Harvest	5	$12.00 ea	$60.00
24	B-82	31 Reasons People Do Not Receive Their Financial Harvest	5	$12.00 ea	$60.00
25	B-91	The Leadership Secrets Of Jesus	6	$10.00 ea	$60.00
26	B-91	The Leadership Secrets Of Jesus	6	$10.00 ea	$60.00
27	B-92	Secrets Of Journey Vol. 1	15	$5.00 ea	$75.00
28	B-93	Secrets Of Journey Vol. 2	15	$5.00 ea	$75.00
29	B-97	The Assignment Vol. 3: The Trials And The Triumph	7	$10.00 ea	$70.00
30	B-98	The Assignment Vol. 4: The Pain And The Passion	7	$10.00 ea	$70.00
31	B-99	Secrets Of The Richest Man Who Ever Lived	6	$10.00 ea	$60.00
32	B-99	Secrets Of The Richest Man Who Ever Lived	6	$10.00 ea	$60.00
33	B-100	Holy Spirit Handbook Vol. 1	8	$10.00 ea	$80.00
34	B-101	The 3 Most Important Things In Your Life	5	$10.00 ea	$50.00
35	B-101	The 3 Most Important Things In Your Life	5	$10.00 ea	$50.00
36	B-104	7 Keys To 1000 Times More	8	$10.00 ea	$80.00
37	B-104	7 Keys To 1000 Times More	8	$10.00 ea	$80.00
38	B-107	The Uncommon Minister Vol. 1	15	$5.00 ea	$75.00
39	B-108	The Uncommon Minister Vol. 2	15	$5.00 ea	$75.00
40	B-114	The Law Of Recognition	5	$10.00 ea	$50.00
41	B-114	The Law Of Recognition	5	$10.00 ea	$50.00
42	B-115	Seeds Of Wisdom On The Secret Place	15	$5.00 ea	$75.00
43	B-116	Seeds Of Wisdom On The Holy Spirit	15	$5.00 ea	$75.00
44	B-117	Seeds Of Wisdom On The Word Of God	15	$5.00 ea	$75.00
45	B-118	Seeds Of Wisdom On Problem Solving	15	$5.00 ea	$75.00
46	B-122	Seeds Of Wisdom On Your Assignment	15	$5.00 ea	$75.00
47	B-127	Seeds Of Wisdom On Goal-Setting	15	$5.00 ea	$75.00
48	B-137	Seeds Of Wisdom On Productivity	15	$5.00 ea	$75.00

Total of 445 Books and Display ~~$3,674.00~~

$1,985.00

THE WISDOM CENTER P.O. Box 99, Denton, Texas 76202

1-888-WISDOM1
(1-888-947-3661)

Website:
WWW.THEWISDOMCENTER.TV

UNCOMMON WISDOM FOR UNCOMMON ACHIEVERS

Dream 7 PAK

- ► **The Leadership Secrets Of Jesus** (B-91 / $10)
- ► **Dream Seeds** (B-11 / $9)
- ► **Secrets Of The Richest Man Who Ever Lived** (B-99 / $10)
- ► **The Assignment: The Dream And The Destiny, Volume 1** (B-74 / $10)
- ► **The Holy Spirit Handbook** (B-100 / $10)
- ► **The Law Of Recognition** (B-114 / $10)
- ► **31 Reasons People Do Not Receive Their Financial Harvest** (B-82 / $12)

The Wisdom Center

7 Books for only $50 $71 Value

WBL-23

Wisdom Is The Principal Thing

Add 10% For S/H

THE WISDOM CENTER
P.O. Box 99, Denton, Texas 76202

1-888-WISDOM1
(1-888-947-3661)

Website:
WWW.THEWISDOMCENTER.TV